COMMUNICATION, SPACE, & DESIGN

The Integral Relation between Communication and Design

Amardo Rodriguez

Hamilton Books
A member of
The Rowman & Littlefield Publishing Group
Lanham · Boulder · New York · Toronto · Oxford

Copyright © 2005 by
Hamilton Books
4501 Forbes Boulevard
Suite 200
Lanham, Maryland 20706
Hamilton Books Acquisitions Department (301) 459-3366

PO Box 317
Oxford
OX2 9RU, UK

Library of Congress Control Number: 2005930789
ISBN 0-7618-3286-6 (paperback : alk. ppr.)

⊖™ The paper used in this publication meets the minimum
requirements of American National Standard for Information
Sciences—Permanence of Paper for Printed Library Materials,
ANSI Z39.48—1984

For those who believe in the possibility of a world without walls.

Table of Contents

Prologue   vii

I. Implications of Physical Fragmentation   1

    Background

    The Economics of Fragmentation

    The Crisis of Communication

    On Being Human

    Final Thoughts

II. Locating the Communication Origins of New Spaces and Designs   13

    Communication as Meaning Creation and Meaning Negotiation

    New Understandings of the World

    Communication and the Jumping Universe

    The Promise of Dialogue and Emergence

    Final Thoughts

III. Locating and Dislocating Community In a Global World   27

    Searching for Community

    Community as a Verb

    The Promise of Community

    Final Thoughts

IV. Searching For New Models of Space in Spanglish   41

     Check Miscellaneous

     Spanglish and Its Critics

     Discussion

     Final Thoughts

V. Department of Homeland Security   53

     The Marriage Between Space and Knowledge

     The Dawning of a New Knowledge

VI. On Fragmentation & Union   67

VII. Space & Ecology   69

VIII. The Walls of the Bible   75

     The Gospels of Matthew Mark, and John

     New Gods and Straight Lines

Epilogue   85

References   87

Index   93

About the Author   95

Prologue

This book explores the relation between our spaces and designs and what being human means. I look at how our spaces and designs relate to matters of democracy, diversity, civility, and other social justice issues. I argue that at the core of our spaces and designs is the need to exercise order and control on the world because we believe the world is in conflict with us. That is, in believing we have to order and control the world to survive and prosper, we posit a deep distrust and suspicion of the world, each other, and our own humanity. Fear, distrust, and suspicion thus permeate our spaces and designs—reflecting and perpetuating our deepest anxieties and insecurities. The result is that our spaces and designs promote separation (as seen, for example, in the redundancy of right-angled walls)—separation between the world and us, and separation between ourselves and others.

I argue that this separation threatens our own well-being, and that of the world, by ripping us from the womb of the world. It extricates us from the natural tensions and rhythms that make for the natural harmony that maintains the world. In this way, this separation deepens our belief that our humanity is separate from the natural world and, as such, our well-being begins and ends with our own interests rather than with the interests of the world and each other. We therefore come to believe that our well-being can be sought without any implication or consequence to the well-being and interests of the world and others.

I contend that separation turns us inward rather than outward, thereby making us more private and less public. We find this increasing inwardness, for instance, in the rise of gated communities, exclusionary suburbs, and hyper-suburbs. I contend that this inward turn ultimately limits our obligation to the world and each other by discouraging us from developing the necessary emotional and spiritual resiliency that comes with interacting and developing complex relations with diverse peoples, such as the peoples we are most likely to encounter in public spaces.

We can, no doubt, organize our spaces to promote union rather than separation. We can have spaces that promote deep and complex relations with the world and each other. We can have spaces that foster trust, openness, and compassion—spaces that expand our humanity by making us less afraid of the world and of each other. We can also have spaces that promote cooperation and mutuality. But the evolution of all these spaces is intertwined with the evolution of a new worldview, a new consciousness of the world. We are now, no doubt, on the cusp of this new worldview. I discuss in this book the promise of this worldview for making new spaces and designs.

Ultimately, the goal of this book is to push forward a theoretical framework that heightens our awareness of the impact of our spaces and designs on the human condition. Moreover, in a world where our distances and spaces are increasingly contracting and collapsing, this framework gives us a reliable means to navigate this emergent world in ways that escape the dread that many fear will come from our collapsing spaces. It also allows us to appreciate the futility that comes with the border walls, such as the one being built in Israel, that more and more nations seem intent on erecting. Further, this theory gives us the means to imagine spaces and designs in bold new ways by promoting new definitions of space and place. It compellingly speaks to human beings as spatial beings by highlighting the role that spaces and designs can potentially play in making us more human. This theory therefore deepens our understanding of what being human means. In the end, I hope this book offers pathways to spaces and designs that make for a more humane world.

I

Implications of Physical Fragmentation

Only when we see ourselves in our true human context, as members of a race intended to be one organism and "one body," will we begin to understand the positive importance not only of the successes but of the failures and accidents in our lives. My successes are not my own. The way to them was prepared by others. The fruit of my labors is not my own: for I am preparing the way for the achievements of another. Nor are my failures my own. They may spring from the failure of another, but they are also compensated for by another's achievement. Therefore the meaning of life is not to be looked for merely in the sum total of my own achievements. It is seen only in the complete integration of my achievements and failures with the achievements and failures of my own generation, and society. . . . Every other man is piece of myself, for I am part and a member of mankind.

Thomas Merton, *No Man Is an Island*

The United States is increasingly being spatially balkanized. As the wealth gap widens between rich and poor, so also the physical division between the groups widens. We increasingly share no common spatial ground. Our spaces and designs are increasingly fragmenting us (Goldsmith & Blakely, 1992; Liggett & Perry, 1995; Massey & Denton, 1993; Phelan & Schneider, 1996; Southworth & Ben-Joseph, 1993; Stoesz, 1996; Wilson, 1991). We no longer have just suburbs and urban districts. We now also have the *hyper-suburb* and the *gated community*.

The hyper-suburb is found beyond the suburbs. It is carved deep within rural districts in the U.S. Its newly-built houses look like castles. Developers often refer to these houses as *McMansions* (Goldberger, 2000). In the hyper-suburb, common spaces, such as side-walks and community centers, are nearly always nonexistent (Blakely & Snyder, 1997; Duany, Plater-Zyberk, & Speck,

2000; Kunstler, 1993; Southworth & Ben-Joseph, 1993). Perfectly manicured lawns extend to the curb. We find a hegemony of private spaces (Duany, Plater-Zyberk, & Speck, 2000; Southworth & Ben-Joseph, 1993).

The rise of affluent suburbs and hyper-suburbs shows the elevation of class in our ethics and politics (Blakely & Snyder, 1997; Boger & Wegner, 1996; Bullard, Grigsby & Lee, 1994; Calmore, 1996; Cook, 1997). The assumption in the hyper-suburb is that the *best* people make for the *best* neighbors, the *best* neighborhoods, and the *best* school districts (Blakely & Snyder, 1997). The hyper-suburb is also about the culling of the suburbs—getting away from the black and brown peoples who are increasingly moving out to the suburbs (Boal, 1978; Caldiera, 1996; Cutler, Glaeser, & Vigdor, 1999; Downs, 1998; Dreier & Moberg, 1996; Farley, 1995; Hwang & Murdock, 1998; Liska, Logan, & Bellair, 1998; Marcuse, 1996, 1997a, 1997b, 1997c; Ross, 2000; South & Crowder, 1998; Thomas, 1995).

But what ultimately results from this balkanization of our society? What is the impact on our politics and ethics? In fact, what is the impact on the human condition? In *Fortress America*, a book that focuses on the rise of the gated community in the U.S., Edward Blakely and Mary Gail Snyder (1997) put the matter the following way: "What is the measure of nationhood when the divisions between the neighborhoods require guards and fences to keep out other citizens? . . . Can this nation fulfill its social contract in the absence of social contact?" (p. 3). Peter Marcuse (1997) uses the term *hypersegregation* when discussing the implications of our increasing physical and spatial fragmentation. Indeed, our increasing spatial separation physically captures our increasing apathy to the plight of the poor, marginalized, and downtrodden.

In what follows, I argue that our increasing physical and spatial separation undermines the evolution of ways of being that are vital to our becoming more human, retards the moral development of our society, and fosters a deep fear and suspicion of others who appear either racially, socially, culturally, or economically different. What emerges is a political and social system that puts us at each other's throats by diminishing our understanding of who and what we are as human beings.

Background

Many persons are writing compellingly about the perilous and pernicious threats to our democracy that our increasing physical and spatial fragmentation poses to U.S. society (Blakely & Snyder, 1997; Boger & Wegner, 1996; Bullard, Grigsby & Lee, 1994; Calmore, 1996; Cutler, Glaeser, & Vigdor, 1999; Dreier, 1996; Duany, Plater-Zyberk, & Speck, 2000; Farley, 1995; Flynn, 1995; Garreau, 1991; Keating, 1994; Liggett & Perry, 1995; Marcuse, 1994, 1996,

1997; Goldsmith & Blakely, 1992; Massey & Denton, 1993; Phelan & Schneider, 1996; Southworth & Ben-Joseph, 1993; Stoesz, 1996; Wilson, 1991). While I use the term *hyper-suburb*, other persons use such terms as *affluent suburb, out-ring suburb, xuburbs, citadels,* and *the totalizing exclusionary suburb.* But all of us generally agree that our increasing physical and spatial fragmentation is making for a society that is increasingly unequal as a result of the concentration of political power in affluent suburbs and the diminution of such power in urban districts.

This new political power is selfishly being used to forward the interests of affluent suburbanites and hyper-suburbanites and directly contributing to the pauperization and ghettoization of urban districts, as the gains that rich suburbs now enjoy are a result of the transfer of resources away from urban districts (Dreier, 1996; Goldsmith & Blakely, 1992; Marcuse, 1994, 1996, 1997; Massey & Denton, 1993; McClain, 1995; Phelan & Schneider, 1996; Wilson, 1991). We have many compelling descriptions of this transfer of resources and the debilitating effects of such transfer on urban districts (e.g., Dreier, 1996; Jencks, 1991; Judd, 1995; Mingione, 1996; Stoesz, 1996; Sugrue, 1996; Wacquant, 1993; Wilson, 1987, 1991). There is a general view that this trend makes for a "deeply divided and very troubled society." Indeed, black, brown, and poor folks are unfortunately bearing the full brunt of this transfer of political power to the suburbs and hyper-suburbs. According to Marcuse (1997), "The residents of ghettos stand in an inferior, generally dominated and exploited (although resisting) relationship to those outside," whereas those in affluent suburbs benefit "disproportionately from their economic and political relationships with others" (p. 315). What is emerging is a new kind of ghettoization that appears bent on keeping black, brown, and poor folks confined to certain spaces that are without any kind of political and social power (McClain, 1995). About this emerging ghetttoization, Marcuse (1997) writes:

> The excluded ghetto of today is not simply an extreme form of the traditional ghetto but a new form in which permanent exclusion from participation in the mainstream economy, whether formal or informal, has become its defining characteristic. The historical changes in the traditional ghetto that have produced the excluded ghetto include a range of contemporary economic forces— from post-Fordist changes in the organization of production to globalization to business activities to development of new informational technologies—and the political and social consequences of these forces interact with entrenched patterns of racial discrimination and spatial segregation. The excluded ghetto is today both the home and the place of work of those whom Wilson (1991) calls the *ghetto poor.* Its characteristics have been often described. It is inseparably linked in the United States to racist patterns. One may thus speak of hyperseg-regation not as identical with exclusion but as very largely overlapping it, and the figures show little or no reduction in its extent despite more than four decades of formal governmental commitment to its abolition. (p. 316)

Indeed, the affluent suburbs and hyper-suburbs are increasingly determining and shaping U.S. politics (Cook, 1997; Dreier & Moberg, 1996; Goldsmith &

Blakely, 1992; Lehrer, 1998; Longman, 1998; Marcuse, 1997a, 1997b, 1997c; Mingione, 1996; Musante, 1998; Wilson, 1987, 1991). Most U.S. residents now live in the suburbs and hyper-suburbs, and this number is rising rapidly (Cook, 1997; Farley, 1995). The result of this outward migration is the redrawing of electoral districts, which is making the suburbs and hyper-suburbs the new power base in U.S. politics. Suburbs now have the most congressional seats of all electoral regions. In fact, in the last two decades, suburban seats have nearly doubled, whereas other regions have significantly declined (Cook, 1997). Finally, suburbanites and hyper-suburbanites vote overwhelmingly for presidents and representatives who have little interests in redeeming urban districts (Goldsmith & Blakely, 1992; Marcuse, 1997; Massey & Denton, 1993). In fact, such presidents and representatives are often hostile to the interests of urban districts (Wilson, 1987, 1991). Paula McClain (1995) writes about a *politics of homicide*:

> An entire generation of black youth is being wiped out, and the issue of urban homicide is not on the governmental agenda in a meaningful way. There is clearly a *politics of homicide*. The politics of homicide results from the use of race in American politics and the image of white victimization by black criminals. The politicization of the problem of urban homicide as one of blacks preying on whites is a nondecision—the mobilization of bias to regard the phenomenon of black against white. The consequence has been to push the development of policies that do not help the true victims of urban violence, urban black residents, but that clearly confront the racial overtones of black-on-white crime. (p. 643)

This hostility to urban districts is best seen in the politics of Ronald Reagan, who achieved nearly total control of the suburban and hyper-suburban vote. Reagan's politics and policy initiatives were particularly harsh on urban districts (Dreier, 1996; Massey & Denton, 1993; Stoesz, 1996; Wilson, 1987, 1991). In Ronald Reagan's politics, the origins of urban blights were seen to be personal rather than structural, therefore needing personal rather than structural solutions. McClain (1995) apply describes Reagan's philosophy regarding urban problems:

> Poverty and associated problems are viewed as a result of individual personal failings and limited intellectual capabilities rather than structural and institutional factors. Government programs and intervention are undesirable and a waste of money. Solutions, if there are any to what they view as fundamentally intractable problems, will emerge from the private sector, and the free market will find them. (pp. 642- 643)

Reagan drastically cut funding for all kinds of urban programs. Even many successful programs were cut by over 70% (Calmore, 1993; Dreier, 1996; Stoesz, 1993). Reagan also completely eliminated general revenue sharing, "which in 1980 had provided $10.8 billion in direct funds to local governments" (Dreier, 1996). In addition, Reagan imposed a huge number of mandates on urban districts, which cost these districts billions of dollars. As Peter Dreier (1996) reports:

> The combined impact of these cuts and mandates has been devastating to the ability of local governments to deliver services and to the capacity of urban residents to cope with poverty and various health, housing, and other problems associated with poverty. Because the number of poor Americans grew significantly during the past decade while concentration of the poor in cities increased, cities experienced the most serious repercussions from the cutbacks and programs designed to serve individuals. The recession, which began in 1989, exacerbated the local fiscal crisis by undermining the capacity of local governments to raise revenues from property taxes (p. 109).

On the other hand, as funding was being cut to urban districts, Reagan was generously allocating funds to suburban districts for highway development, public works, and other infrastructure projects. This support was, and remains, vital to the expansion of hyper-suburbs (Lehrer, 1998; Longman, 1998). The allocation of federal funds to build new highways, rather than expand mass transit systems, is also significant. According to Joe Persky, "It's all a matter of people not seeing the right price. In many cases, governments are subsidizing highway construction over mass transit and doing all sorts of other things that result in people paying too little for the resources they use; the result is sprawl and traffic congestion and it's becoming a major problem" (quoted in Lehrer, 1998). Other costs can be found in the pollution that comes with the increasing miles being traveled between home and work in larger vehicles, the degradation to the environment that comes with the increasing pollution, the physical heath problems that come with this increased pollution, the allocation of limited funds to protect land areas so as to control hyper-suburban development, and the loss of prime farm land to suburban and hyper-suburban development (Duany, Plater-Zyberk, & Speck, 2000; Jackson, 1985; Massey & Denton, 1993; O'Meara, 1999).

Our increasing physical fragmentation demands a psychology that disconnects us from the suffering of those left behind in ghettos and barrios. Our supposed *success* requires psychological legitimization in a political system that must also produce losers. If our success is deserved because of our efforts and dedication, then the failure of the poor is deserved because of their lack of effort and dedication. So the identity of many poor people is increasingly being defined in terms of failure. This rhetorical strategy allows us to mask the deep ideological, political, cultural, and racial structures that are making for the widening gap between rich and poor. As Ellen Goodman (1984) observes, "If we are going to limit opportunities for those stuck in the Other America, it is much easier to think of these people as failures. If we are going to chip away at social programs for the have-nots, it is much easier to name them losers. We used to call this blaming the victim. Now we call it winning" (p. 5).

The politics that is emerging out of our increasing spatial separation is working in tandem with an emerging economics that is also legitimizing and encouraging separation and fragmentation.

The Economics of Fragmentation

This emergent economics is dedicated to the "unleashing of market forces" and privileging the interests of elites of wealth and power. It is determined to end all political and social practices that supposedly *bridle* the power of capitalism. It is also committed to the evolution of capitalism and, accordingly, against any government that is undedicated to the full expansion of capitalism. Capitalism is, presumably, the only path to the *good society*. For instance, George Will (1995) writes:

> A society that values individualism, enterprise and a market economy is neither surprised nor scandalized when the unequal distribution of marketable skills produces large disparities in the distribution of wealth. This does not mean that social justice must be defined as whatever distribution of wealth the market produces. But it does mean there is a presumption in favor of respecting the market's version of distributive justice. Certainly there is today no prima facie case against the moral acceptability of increasingly large disparities of wealth. (p. A15)

George Will and company work with the assumption that human beings have a proclivity for devolution, chaos, and death, and that competition is the natural order of the world. Supposedly, capitalism gives us the superior mechanisms and structures to control our proclivity for destruction and anarchy. In fact, capitalism presumably harnesses this proclivity for the good of all human beings. The competition that capitalism fosters supposedly makes for the constructive playing out of our supposed natural yearning for aggression, competition, and destruction. Supposedly, without capitalism this aggression will be channeled towards destructive ends. As such, capitalism supposedly makes for the most productive use of human and natural resources and, in so doing, makes for the good society. *The Wall Street Journal* editorializes endlessly about the veracity of these claims.

Thomas Sowell (1994) also argues that capitalism undercuts discrimination. Discrimination undercuts the promise of competition. Winning demands the acquisition of the best persons, regardless of race, ethnicity, sexual orientation, and so forth. In fact, many persons of historically disenfranchised and marginalized groups are increasingly the most vociferous proponents of this argument. This argument is often showcased as a compelling reason that explains why liberalism is supposedly dead. Capitalism is supposedly the "crowning achievement" of Western civilization, and the full commitment of the U.S. to capitalism makes for the "unsurpassed greatness" of the U.S. George Gilder (1981) even claims that capitalism is an outgrowth of our spiritual evolution. It reflects our spiritual questing for a society that will unleash all of our potentiality. Simply put, capitalism is of God. It supposedly constitutes the only society that God blesses. Consequently, to be against capitalism is, supposedly, to be against God; and, as such, to be against capitalism is to face the wrath of God. Gilder and company often use this reasoning to explain the downfall of socialism and communism.

The economics of the hyper-suburbs is therefore against the redistribution of wealth and resources. These practices supposedly only sponsor government programs and initiatives that stop the poor and downtrodden from developing the *superior* habits of being that make for a better life in a capitalist system (see Dawkins, 1989; Liebmann, 1999; Mansfield, 1996; Wilson, 1978; R. Wright, 1994; W. Wright, 1998). In other words, such programs supposedly undercut the evolution of our preservation instincts. The economics of affluent suburbs and hyper-suburbs champions the power of self-interest. The mansion in the hyper-suburb is the promised reward of self-interest. It stands as testimony that capitalism offers a paradigm that transcends race, ethnicity, and class history. Any person who exercises the highest levels of self-interest, regardless of race, ethnicity, or gender, can supposedly have the rewards of capitalism. In this way, hyper-suburbs reflect the evolution of the good society. It is supposedly collective interests—such as civil rights, unions, and identity politics—that bedevil the evolution of the good society. Thus the economics—as well as the politics—of the hyper-suburbs is openly committed to eroding the power of unions and other interest groups that press the interests of historically marginalized and disenfranchised peoples; most of whom, of course, are left behind in urban districts.

For Will, Sowell, Gilder, and company, hierarchy is the natural order of the world. The elites of wealth and power, as Richard Herrnstein and Charles Murray discuss in *The Bell Curve: Intelligence and Class Structure in American Life*, are simply biologically advantaged to rise to the top of society. In this regard, the hyper-suburbs supposedly reflect *just* rewards. The economics of the hyper-suburbs is against social programs and initiatives that reject the supposed *truths* of biology. Such efforts apparently work against the natural order of the world. Accordingly, the economics and politics of the hyper-suburbs are strenuously against new school funding systems that make for parity between rich and poor school districts, as well as other initiatives and programs that aim to expand opportunity and access to persons of historically marginalized and disenfranchised groups. In the end, the economics of the hyper-suburbs assumes that self-interest, selfishness, competition, and hierarchy will ultimately make for the good society. In reality, however, the economics and politics that are emerging out of our increasing physical and spatial fragmentation harm our own moral evolution. This harm can be aptly seen in our increasing *crisis of communication* (Buber, 1970; Cissna & Anderson, 1994; Rodriguez, 2003).

The Crisis of Communication

Communication is fundamentally a relational phenomenon—through communication relationships are constituted, shaped, and managed, and through communication our humanity is negotiated, shaped, and defined. As McNamee and Gergen (1999) note, "It is out of relationships that we develop meanings, rationalities, the sense of value, moral interest, motivation, and so on" (p. 10). Thus to speak about the deterioration of communication is to speak to ways of being in the world that diminish our relationships, that undercut meaning creation, that block the evolution of new and different ways of experiencing the world, and that undermine the deepening and expansion of our relationships to the world, each other, and our own humanity. Such ways of being are devoid of empathy, compassion, transparency, and trust; which is to say that such ways of being are laden with apathy, deception, suspicion, and distrust. The result of such ways of being is alienation.

Alienation dispossesses life of meaning, passion, and purpose by disconnecting action from meaning (Fromm, 1973). It undermines our ability to act deliberately and purposefully upon the world. It fosters despair by mystifying our power to alter and control our realities. In this way, alienation heightens our fear of the world, each other, and our own humanity. Ronald Arnett (1994) contends that our losing faith in our ability to act upon the world makes for despair, mistrust, confusion, loss of moral direction, and what Lasch (1984) refers to as a "culture of survivalism."

Erich Fromm contends that alienation is the hallmark of separation. It reduces us to objects by undermining our ability to act upon the world. It also dehumanizes us by disentangling our humanity from the humanity of others. In *Anatomy of Human Destructiveness*, Fromm (1973) writes:

> Alienation as we find it in modern society is almost total; it pervades the relationship of man to his work, to the things he consumes, to the state, to his fellow man, and to himself. Man has created a world of man-made things as it never existed before. He has constructed a complicated social machine to administer the technical machine he built. Yet this whole creation of his stands over and above him. He does not feel himself as a creator and center, but as the servant of a Golem, which his hands have built. The more powerful and gigantic the forces are which he unleashes, the more powerless he feels himself as a human being. He confronts himself with his own forces embodied in things he has created, alienated from himself. He is owned by his own creation, and has lost ownership of himself. (pp. 124-125)

High density living expands communication organically. Tight proximity forces us to develop a communication temperament in order to deal with all kinds of people. Communication is compulsory. We have to constantly negotiate all kinds of relationships, with all different kinds of people. Prosperity depends on our ability to get along. We have to be willing to share resources, make compromises, tolerate differences, build and rebuild coalitions, forgive past hurts and injustices, and ease tensions and conflicts. The hyper-suburb and the gated community make no such demands on us. In fact, the hyper-suburb is *meant* to make no such demands on us. It purposely turns us inward (private) rather than outward (public); thus the absence of sidewalks, front porches, parks, community centers, and playgrounds. Huge lawns also maintain separation and fragmentation between neighbors, and street arrangement discourages entry of nonresidents (Southworth & Ben-Joseph, 1993).

The huge houses in the hyper-suburbs show the rise of a disturbing materialism in U.S. society. Yet the rise of this materialism aptly captures our crisis of meaning by reflecting a grasping for meaning, any meaning. The huge houses in the hyper-suburbs stand as the houses of worship to the new religion of materialism. We now each have our own house of worship. We have no need for fellowship with others. But the dominant spiritual teachings of the world consistently teach us that redemption is about expanding our humanity, forging new and different ways of being and experiencing the world, and deepening our relations to each other. Love of God is about love of others. As Duany, Plater-Zyberk, and Speck (2000) note, "The unity of society is threatened not by the use of gates but the uniformity and exclusivity of the people behind them. . . . A child growing up in such a homogenous environment is less likely to develop a sense of empathy for people from other walks of life and is ill prepared to live in a diverse society. The *other* becomes alien to the child's experience, witnessed only through the sensationalizing eye of the television" (pp. 45-46).

On Being Human

Hyper-suburbs and gated-communities thrive on the belief that security can be found by establishing rigid enclaves far away from ghettos and barrios. Both assume that our redemption can be disassociated from the redemption of those persons who are trapped in ghettos and barrios. Security is cast in terms of physical safety: it can supposedly be acquired with enough walls, enough fences, and enough gates. That is, security is defined in terms of protection from injury to body and property. But what about spiritual injury? What about injury to community? What about injury to our humanity? What about injury to the planet? What protection and security do hyper-suburbs and gated-communities offer against such injuries? In fact, what of the exponentially high illicit drug and alcohol use among suburban children, along with the high levels of suicide, the high levels of human misery and anguish, and the high levels of promiscuity? Suburban children are unfortunately, and sadly, paying a lot of the cost for our fixation on physical security. The numerous shootings in affluent schools make this plain to us. The physical security that the suburbs and hyper-suburbs supposedly offer does nothing to stop all of this misery. The point is that our focus on physical safety distracts us from the work of creating worlds that are really safe. What ultimately matters is spiritual security—safety from fear, suspicion, distrust, despair, hopelessness, and apathy. This security only evolves with the evolution of community. As such, no amount of money or walls or fences or gates can give us this security.

But the children in the ghettos and barrios are also hurting. Because the building of suburbs and hyper-suburbs transfers money and resources out of urban districts, urban housing and schools are left under-funded. The tremendous political clout of the suburbs guarantees the continuation of this unjust system. So the children of the ghettos and barrios are left to "thrive" in housing and schools that are unfit, even for animals (Kozol, 1992). To deal with the obvious hypocrisy of all of this, suburbanites and hyper-suburbanites back a politics of competition and voucher programs for urban schools, neither of which can be found in suburban schools. The fact that suburban schools are simply better funded never enters any equation (Fischer et al., 1996; Kozol, 1992). Unfortunately, suburbanites and hyper-suburbanites continue to get away with this politics.

The reality is that hyper-suburbanites look at black, brown, and poor children as *other* children. The media coverage of suburban school shootings demonstrates this well. Such violence is supposedly unnatural in affluent suburban neighborhoods. It is, however, supposedly natural in poor school districts. We are to believe that black, brown, and poor parents make no effort to raise decent, kind, and generous children. Consequently, reports of black, brown, and poor children killing each other never get comparable media attention (Patterson, 1999). Our disowning of black, brown, and poor children is also seen in our politics. Besides actually demanding programs for urban schools that are nonexistent in affluent suburban schools, the politics of the suburbs and hyper-suburbs is opposed to even any suggestion of ending a school funding system that works against the interest and betterment of poor schools and opposed to other initiatives that can positively affect the lives of many black, brown, and poor children. Obviously, there is something morally depraved about this politics. Yet, on the other hand, this politics reflects so much about us. It captures our alienation and fragmentation, and, most of all, our moral devolution. The fact that race, ethnicity, and class can stop us from loving other children as our own should concern us deeply. This reality reflects an impoverished and diminished humanity. Orlando Patterson (1999) editorializes this point well in the wake of another suburban school shooting:

> What is at issue here is the principle of infrangibility: our conception of normalcy and of what groups constitute our social body—those from whom we cannot be separated without losing our identity, so that their achievements become our own and their pathologies our failures. We should speak not simply of black poverty but of the nation's poverty; not the Italian-American Mafia problem but the nation's organized crime problem; not the pathologies of privileged white teen-age boys but of all our unloved, alienated young men.

The condition of our humanity will always be measured by our treatment of the weak and the innocent. As such, viewing black, brown, and poor children as *other* children signals a high level of moral devolution.

Final Thoughts

We are increasingly engaged in a politics that encourages reform rather than revolution. The result is a consideration of only those solutions that pose no threat to the status quo; that is, solutions that really demand nothing from us. Case in point: many now contend that the solution to urban school problems is voucher programs, and the solution to our growing criminal and deviant problems is incarceration, and the solution to the growing chasm between rich and poor is tax relief, and the solution to our youth problems is the posting of the Ten Commandments in schools, and the solution to our suburban problems is the construction of new and wider highways, and the solution to our diversity problem is immigration laws, and so forth. This reactionary approach makes for a psychology and sociology that distort our identity as human beings that belong to one and the same life world. It ultimately distorts our understanding of what being human means by masking our potentiality. In other words, no amount of walls, fences, and gates will save us from the perils of a politics that fosters fragmentation, division, and separation. We urgently need a new politics and ethics.

II

Locating the Communication Origins of New Spaces and Designs

If we understand that design leads to the manifestation of human intention, and if what we make with our hand is to be sacred and honor the earth that gives us life, then the things we make must not only rise from the ground but return to it, soil to soil, water to water, so everything that is received from the earth can be freely given back with out causing harm to any living system. This is ecology. This is good design. It is of this we must now speak.

William McDonough, *Design, Ecology, Ethics and the Making of Things*

Our spaces and designs are ideologically laden (Bachelard, 1994; Castells, 2000; Foucault, 1980; Grosz, 2001; Harvey, 1990, 2000; Jameson, 1991; Jencks, 1977, 1997; Soja, 1989; Venturi, Brown, & Izenour, 1977; Weisman, 1994). Both reflect, reinforce, and perpetuate our deepest beliefs, fears, suspicions, assumptions, hopes, and truths about the world. In *Discrimination by Design*, Leslie Kanes Weisman (1994) contends that "Space, like language, is socially constructed, and like the syntax of language, the spatial arrangements of our buildings and communities reflect and reinforce the nature of gender, race, and class relations in society." Thus, "the uses of both language and space contribute to the power of some groups over others and the maintenance of human inequality" (p. 2). Indeed, behind our spaces and design—in the Western world—is the belief that we have to coercively order and control the world in order to survive and prosper. Accordingly, our buildings stand as conquest, challenging the natural world to contest our dominance and control over it. Still, as Shome (2003) notes, "The role of space in the production of cultural power and politics has been largely ignored in cultural theory and criticism, with the exception of geography and, more recently, anthropology. For the most part, space tends to be acknowledged to the extent that we are able to recognize different social and cultural patterns in different spaces or to the extent that we see space as a background, a backdrop against which the real stuff of history and politics are enacted" (p. 39).

Charles Jencks (1977) acknowledges that architecture needs a new theory of communication so as to give us a new way to articulate the signs, symbols, and meanings of our spaces and designs. He believes that such a theory can be found in semiotics. Semiotics supposedly provides a sign system that gives us a language to articulate the meanings of our spaces and designs. Our buildings would no longer lack meanings.

> *We must go back to a point where architects took responsibility for rhetoric, for how their buildings communicated intentionally . . . and then combine insights from such a study with a relevant theory of semiotics, so that an updated rhetoric can be consciously taught along with other specialities—no, as the unifying agent of these other disciplines. For an architect's primary and final role is to express the meanings a culture finds significant, as well as elucidate certain ideas and feelings that haven't previously reached expression. The jobs that too often take up his energy might be better done by engineers and sociologists, but no other profession is specifically responsible for articulating meaning and seeing that the environment is sensual, humorous, surprising and coded as a readable text. This is the architect's job and pleasure.*

Charles Jencks   *The language of*
Post-modern Architecture

But, according to Hans Ibelings (1998), semiotics "have made little lasting contribution to architectural criticism and history" (p. 14). "Over the past twenty years, the notion that architecture can to a large extent be understood as a communicative system has become an *idée reçue*. Just what a building can communicate, apart from the fact that it exists, is an open question for which there are dozens of possible answers" (pp. 14-18). Edward Soja (1989) raises a more damning criticism of the use of semiotics in architectural criticism. He writes, "To seek to interpret spatiality from the purview of socially independent processes of semiotic representation is . . . inappropriate and misleading, for it tends to bury social origins and potential social transformation under a distorting screen of idealism and psychologism, a universalized and edenic human nature prancing about in a spaceless and timeless world" (pp. 122-123). Indeed, semiotics is fraught with numerous problems as a communication theory. We need a communication theory that can help us set off a completely different relation to the world and each other—one, of course, that promotes a more collaborative approach to the world. In other words, semiotics gives us no new ontological foundation to look anew at the relation between being human and the conception of our spaces and designs. It perpetuates the belief that there is no moral, existential, or spiritual relation between our spaces and designs and us. As such, semiotics gives us no moral or theoretical foundation to either examine or understand the implications of our spaces and designs on the human condition and that of the world. It lacks the theoretical power we now so desperately need to grapple with a complex and perilous set of world issues.

In my view, the evolution of new models of spaces and designs is dependent on the evolution of a more constitutive understanding of communication; that is, a meaning-oriented and relational understanding of communication. Integral to such an understanding of communication are the notions that communication is foremost a relational phenomenon—through communication we are either building or undermining our relationships with the world, each other, and ourselves, and that our relationships recursively shape our humanity. In this way, communication locates us in the world. A constitutive understanding of communication therefore helps us to better situate discussions of space and design within a more heuristic communication and rhetorical theory, and, in so doing, helps us to better appreciate the impact of our designs on our various relational worlds.

Communication as Meaning Creation and Meaning Negotiation

We must face the fact that what we are seeing across the world today is war, a war against life itself. Our present systems of design have created a world that grows far beyond the capacity of the environment to sustain life into the future. The industrial idiom of design, failing to honor the principles of nature, can only violate them, producing waste and harm, regardless of purported intention. If we destroy more forests, burn more garbage, drift-net more fish, burn more coal, bleach more paper, destroy more topsoil, poison more insects, build over more habitats, dam more rivers, produce more toxic and radioactive wastes, we are creating a vast industrial machine, not for living in, but for dying in. It is a war, to be sure, a war that only a few more generations can surely survive . . . . We have to recognize that every event and manifestation of nature is "design," that to live within the laws of nature means to express our human intention as an interdependent species, aware and grateful that we are at the mercy of sacred forces larger than ourselves, and that we obey these laws in order to honor the sacred in each other and in all things. We must come to peace with and accept our place in the natural world.

William McDonough, *Design, Ecology,
Ethics and the Making of Things*

We commonly assume that the origins of communication reside in necessity, utility, and functionality. It is informational in nature and psychological and biological in origin. Supposedly, communication is a tool, an instrument that evolved out of our evolutionary need for superior forms of coordination and organization. We assume no moral, existential, and spiritual relation between communication and being human, or between communication and the world.

Besides mastery of various skills and techniques that allow for clarity of thought and expression, communication supposedly demands nothing of us. We use communication and information interchangeably. We believe that new spaces and designs with, for example, less walls and right-angles, will automatically increase communication and, in so doing, increase productivity and creativity. We can therefore supposedly improve communication by merely manipulating our spaces and designs. Suffice it to say, Lee Thayer's observation remains compelling: "I am convinced that our failure to see communication for what it is—the source of our humanity and of everything else that is human—is not purely an intellectual shortcoming but a moral one."

We assume our spaces and designs come with no moral, existential, and spiritual implications because our common understanding of communication points to no such implications. Consequently, we assume that our spaces and designs have no implications for the condition of our humanity, much less for the condition of the world. In other words, the organization of our spaces and designs is inherently depoliticized because our understanding of communication is inherently depoliticized. Thus new conceptions of spaces and designs that remain beholden to an understanding of communication that locates the origins of communication in necessity and utility pose no threat to the status quo and, therefore, give us new no possibilities of being in the world with each other. To come to genuinely new conceptions of spaces and designs demands that we look anew at what being human means, and this ultimately involves looking anew at the origins of communication and the relation between communication and being human. In fact, to look anew at communication ultimately demands looking anew at the world, and this, of course, is never easy. But this work has already begun and new understandings of communication are emerging. This project, for example, is aptly captured in the title of a paper by Vernon Cronen: "Communication Theory for the 21st Century: Cleaning up the Wreckage of the Psychology Project." Cronen (1998) contends that psychologically based—that is, transmission oriented—models of communication—which, again, are the dominant models in communication studies—undermine the study of social life by, among other things, downplaying the role of social forces in shaping self-hood, promoting a representational view of language, disconnecting "attention, perception, and recall from the process of communication," obscuring the interactive making of social problems, "assuming that individuality is a property of persons," inhibiting constructive political and institutional change by encouraging "us to look for the solution to most every problem inside individuals' minds," and rendering cultural differences either intractable or trivial by "treating meaning as individuals' command of a cultural code" (pp. 22-27).

We are increasingly recognizing that communication is the constitutive element of being human. It is about the creation and negotiation of meaning so as to attain mutual understanding. Communication is first and foremost about meanings, relationships, and presences. In being the constitutive element of our humanity, communication shapes our humanity. It is thereby inherently moral, existential, and political. To look at communication as the constitutive process of being human politicizes the organization of our spaces and designs. Just as much as no communication is ever politically and ethically neutral (the reason, again, being that all communication practices either promote or undermine the evolution of our humanity), so our spaces and designs, in being inherently rhetorical, always come with political and moral implications. In other words, some communication practices constitute us better than others and, accordingly, help make for more humane and just worlds than others. We need only note the damaged humanity of children in many impoverished orphanages throughout the world, who were deprived of caring and nurturing communication environs and relationships, to help make this point.

We now make a distinction between definitions of communication that stress expression and transmission and emergent definitions that stress negotiation and collaboration. The first set of definitions encourages us to look at communication in terms of strategy and techniques (e.g., "How To Win Friends And Influence People"). Presumably, *good* communication demands commonality in our symbols and codes. Moreover, ambiguity, diversity, and complexity presumably threaten communication. As such, the goal is to remove such elements and pollutants from our meanings, understandings, and relationships. We promote communication as expression and transmission through spaces and designs that limit the intensity of communication by suppressing conflict, dissent, and diversity.

> *That peoples can no longer carry on authentic dialogue with one another is not only the most acute symptom of the pathology of our time, it is also that which most urgently makes a demand of us. I believe, despite all, that the peoples in this hour can enter into dialogue, into a genuine dialogue with one another. In a genuine dialogue each of the partners, even when he stands in opposition to the other, heeds, affirms, and confirms his opponent as an existing other. Only so can conflict certainly not be eliminated from the world, but be humanly arbitrated and led towards it's overcoming.*

> Martin Buber, *Genuine Dialogues and*
> *the Possibility of Peace*

Dialogue, on the other hand, looks at communication as, fundamentally, a way of being that emphasizes openness, affirmation, and compassion. It focuses on "the quality of relationship between or among two or more people and the communication acts that create and sustain that relationship." It also reflects, as Cissna and Anderson (1994) point out, "the attitudes participants bring to an encounter, the ways they talk and act toward one another, the consequences of meeting, and the larger context within which dialogue occurs" (p. 15). In other words, dialogue encourages the embodying of communication and appeals to the moral rather than the primal dimension of our humanity. According to Anderson, Cissna and Arnett (1994), "Dialogue is a dimension of communication quality that keeps communicators more focused on mutuality and relationship than on self interest, more concerned with discovering than with disclosing, more interested in access than in domination" (p. 2).

Dialogue assumes that communication is ultimately about our questing for communion, the recognition of our own humanity in each other. It also assumes that human beings quest for completion, that human beings have the capacity to act deliberately upon the world, that human beings become human only through dialogue, that an existential and spiritual relation exists between human beings and the world, and that the world is incomplete rather than imperfect (Buber, 1970; Cissna & Anderson, 1994, Freire, 1993). Dialogue therefore assumes that the ability to bring forth the world through meaning creation and negotiation. Our becoming is intertwined with that of the world. Communication practices that affirm our becoming also affirm the becoming of the world. In this way, dialogue is both inherently life affirming and moral.

> *Dialogue cannot exist . . . in the absence of a profound love for the world and people. The naming of the world, which is an act of creation and re-creation, is not possible if it is not infused with love. Love is at the same time the foundation of dialogue and dialogue itself. . . . On the other hand, dialogue cannot exist without humility. The naming of the world, through which people constantly re-create that world, cannot be an act of arrogance. . . . How can I dialogue if I am afraid of being displaced, the mere possibility causing me torment and weakness? . . . . Dialogue further requires an intense faith in humankind, faith in their power to make and remake, to create and recreate, faith in their vocation to be more fully human. . . . Faith in people is an a priori requirement for dialogue . . . . Founding itself upon love, humility, and faith, dialogue becomes a horizontal relationship of which mutual trust between dialoguers is the logical consequence.*
>
> Paulo Freire, *Pedagogy of the Oppressed*

To look at communication as the constitutive element of being human, that is, as about our questing for communion and union through mutual understanding, gives us a rich theoretical language with which we can understand, analyze, and critique our spaces and designs. It allows us to make a rigorous distinction between monologic and dialogic spaces and designs. The result is a new set of questions to consider as we engage in discussions about human potentiality. Do our spaces and designs promote trust, compassion, openness, and mutual understanding? Do our spaces and designs promote the full expression of our differences and encourage the evolution of new and different ways of understanding and being in the world? Do our designs and spaces make us less afraid of the world and each other and, as a result, lessen the threat of our differences? Ultimately, do our spaces and designs promote fragmentation and separation or union and communion?

New Understandings of the World

New conceptions of communication are evolving out of and alongside new understandings of the world. Such understandings are releasing us from our distrust and suspicion of the world's ambiguity, diversity, and complexity. For instance, emerging sciences and theories are compellingly suggesting that there is no inherent and intractable conflict between the world and us. Instead, the world seems infinite in nature, which means that no meaning, no understanding, and no truth is ever complete and finite. In other words, the world is inherently interpretive and collaborative—it invites the evolution of new meanings, new interpretations, new understandings. Accordingly, dialogue stresses negotiation, interpretation, and collaboration. It emphasizes openness, compassion, affirmation, and continuity because only such practices promote negotiation, interpretation, and, ultimately, mutual understanding. Dialogue also assumes that diversity, rather than homogeneity, is the order of the world. It disabuses us of the notion that commonality of language is prerequisite for communication. The reality is that communication precedes and exceeds language. Lack of a common language is no impediment to mutual understanding as long as both actors are willing to expend the necessary effort to genuinely negotiate and collaborate. Mutual understanding emerges only through collaboration and negotiation. Thus communication is fundamentally a relational, rather than a symbolic, phenomenon; which is to say that communication is ontological rather than epistemological in nature. It fundamentally locates us in the world, rather than merely inform us about the world. Moreover, in highlighting the relational dimension of our being, new understandings of communication are merely reflecting emergent understandings of the world that show us as fundamentally relational beings belonging to a relational world. As Hugh Prather observes, "Nothing, including me, exists by itself—this is an illusion of words. I am a relationship, ever changing."

David Bohm, who is acknowledged as one of the foremost physicists of the twentieth century, wrote extensively about the nature of dialogue. In *On Dialogue*, Bohm (1996) wrote that dialogue was our only way to end the fragmentation that permeates our being and is responsible for so much misery and suffering in the world. Bohm believed that fragmentation originates in our thought system. He argued that thought, perception, representation, and communication are intertwined and inseparable. Even our best understandings of the world will be incomplete. No system of inquiry will therefore ever possess an absolute and complete understanding of the world. We will never be able to mirror the world. The world and its truths will always be larger than us. We therefore have no business acting like gods or pretending to know the mind of our gods. To understand the world demands humility and openness to other understandings. As Bohm (1996) notes, "How can you share if you are sure you have the truth and the other fellow is sure he has the truth, and the truths don't agree? How can you share?" (p. 37). Dialogue is therefore more concerned with how we approach the world and less concerned with what we claim to know about the world.

> *If we can suspend carrying out our impulses, suspend our assumptions, and look at them all, then we are in the same state of consciousness. And therefore we have established the thing that many people say they want—a common consciousness. It may not be very pleasant, but we have got it. . . . We have to share the consciousness that we actually have. We can't just impose another one. But if people can share the frustration and share their different contradictory assumptions and share their mutual anger and stay with it—if everybody is angry together, and looking at it together—than you have a common consciousness.*

> David Bohm, *On Dialogue*

Bohm also believed that dialogue was the path to understanding the nature of the world. He saw the world as being inherently dialogic. Through dialogue we understand the unfolding nature of the world and that of our own humanity. Dialogue also demands a lot from us because the world demands a lot from us. Dialogue demands the suspension of our deepest assumptions and impulses so that we ebb and flow to the world's quantum rhythms. It also demands the promotion of empathy, openness, continuity, and affirmation, and the development of a rigorous mental, emotional, sensual, and spiritual constitution so as to withstand the complexity, ambiguity, and diversity that come with an everunfolding world. Most importantly, dialogue demands that we locate ourselves differently in relation to the world. We are bound up in this world and this world is bound up in us. In ripping us from the world, separation and fragmentation harm both the world and us. Bohm believed that we could return to a position of union and communion with the world by ending *literal thought* and promoting *participatory thought*. Whereas literal thought assumes separation between the world and us and strives for a description of the world as *it is*, participatory thought assumes no such separation and therefore aims for no such description. It recognizes the relational nature of the world. Dialogue and participatory thought thus share a recursive relation. Through dialogue we promote participatory thought and through participatory thought we promote dialogue. Our responsibility is thus to guard against those thought systems and communication practices that promote separation and fragmentation.

Communication and the Jumping Universe

In *The Architecture of the Jumping Universe*, Charles Jencks (1997) writes about how emergent understandings of the world are making for a new worldview informing our conceptions of space and design. Central to this new worldview is "the idea that the universe is a single, unfolding self-organizing event, something more like an animal than a machine, something radically interconnected and creative, an entity that jumps suddenly to higher levels of organization and delights us as it does so" (p. 125). Jencks contends that this new worldview is releasing us from the dogmatism and atomism of modernism, and the relativism and nihilism of postmodernism, by pointing us to a world laden with beauty, symmetry, and meaning. He also discusses how this emergent worldview is pushing us to reckon architecturally with the planet's ecology.

But Jencks still misses the communication component and, with that, the human element. For instance, Jencks' criteria for architecture make no mention of the need to create spaces and designs that enlarge the human element. He continues to stress aesthetics over ethics. "A new shared language of expression is growing, an aesthetic of undulating movement, of surprising, billowing crystals, fractured planes, and spiraling growth, of wave-forms, twist and folds—a language more in tune with the unfolding, jumping cosmos than the rigid structures of the past" (p. 13). Unfortunately, we find no discussion of how emergent understandings of the world can lend to the evolution of genuinely new conceptions of space and design that can help the world and us unfold in new and exciting ways by promoting union and communion. The many designs and buildings that Jencks discusses—most of which are stunning and fabulous—in order to exemplify the new worldview evidence no such concerns. Yet emergent understandings of the world give most weight to the relation between the condition of our humanity and the conception of our spaces and designs by vividly showing the perils of fragmentation and separation. It was quantum theory, after all, that brought Bohm to dialogue.

Jencks contends that we need to embrace and celebrate our striving to learn. He believes that this striving is our most powerful striving and is what most distinguishes us from other species. But as Paulo Freire explains in *Pedagogy of the Oppressed*, no learning occurs outside of dialogue. Learning outside of dialogue is merely instruction, and instruction does nothing for us. It is the dialogic nature of learning that makes learning such a profound human striving and such an integral component to our liberation. As such, if we really want to promote and celebrate learning, we must promote and celebrate dialogue, and this will involve creating spaces and designs that promote and celebrate dialogue.

Indeed, as Jencks observes, emergent understandings of the world are revealing a world that encourages learning by its being inherently and infinitely interpretive. Such a world enlarges us by promoting inquiry and new understandings. Hope rather than fear finds purchase in such a world. As Bohm observed, emergent understandings of the world point to a dialogic world, and such a world requires that we embody dialogue in our ways of perceiving, relating, understanding, and moving. Through dialogue we find harmony in the form of union and communion with the world and with each other. Unfortunately, as seen in the case of Jencks, we continue to miss or downplay the full implications and consequences of this emergent worldview that is now upon us. So, again, what excites Jencks is the new aesthetics, rather than the new ethics, that this worldview promotes. But our spaces and designs have a profound impact on what it means to be human. Both reflect, reinforce, and perpetuate our deepest beliefs, fears, suspicions, assumptions, hopes, and truths of the world, and, as such, shape how we interact with the world, each other, and even ourselves.

We inhabit our spaces and designs as much as our spaces and designs inhabit us. Thus to fully embody all the implications and consequences of this emergent worldview requires that we be ready to completely reconceptualise our spaces and designs. But as with any revolution, cooptation looms. Cooptation allows us to treat an emergent worldview as merely an emergent perspective. It releases us of the necessary risking of life that comes with a new worldview. No doubt—completely reconceptualizing our spaces and designs demands a lot from us. New spaces and designs will help promote, among other things, new conceptions of who we are, which will make for new and different ways of perceiving, understanding, and relating to others, and new conceptions about our place in the world and the cosmos. As much as identity is social in nature, it is ontological in origin.

The Promise of Dialogue and Emergence

We continue to be seduced by writings and images that tell us that emerging technologies will collapse our common understandings of time and space, and that this disintegration will recursively produce radically new conceptions of self, identity, and society. Science fiction writers, of course, have long been having the most fun with this subject. In the best scenarios, we will supposedly have futures that promise fascinating states of liberation; in the worse scenarios, we will have futures that damn us to the most debilitating kinds of oppression. Actually, the forecasting of how emerging technologies will alter our conceptions of self, identity, and society is a rapidly growing industry, and Manuel Castells (1997, 1998, 2000) is widely acknowledged, especially by those in academe, to be the most important analyst. His trilogy on the *Information Age* is indeed a significant piece of scholarship.

In Castells' forecast, the future offers cause for both despair and hope—a "world troubled by its own promise." Power will no longer be concentrated in institutions (the state), organizations (capitalist firms), and cultural centers (local media, churches). Instead, power will be "diffused in global networks of wealth, power, information and images, which circulate and transmute in a system of variable geometry and dematerialized geography" (Castells, 1997, p. 359). Emerging technologies will make for the fullest expression of capitalism. Elites will continue to use emerging technologies to exact unparalleled levels of subordination and oppression, by finally releasing identity from geography and history and acquiring the means to subject us to the most rigorous kinds of *disciplining.* Also, emerging technologies will create a new kind of virtual space that brings people together and separates them at the same time. This *space of flow* will make for a *real virtuality* that will be characterized by *timeless time* and *placeless space.* According to Castells (2000), "The dominant tendency is toward a horizon of networked, ahistorical space of flows, aiming at imposing its logic over scattered, segmented places, increasingly unrelated to each other, less and less able to share cultural codes" (p. 459).

Castells' thesis is that elites are socially and politically determined to amass global power by "superseding the logic of any specific place" so as to escape "the socio-political control of historically specific local/national societies" (p. 446). What emerges is a social domination where the cultural codes of the elites are "embedded in the social structure in such a way that the possession of these codes opens the access to the power structure without [elites] needing to conspire to bar access to its network" (p. 447). One manifestation of this domination is the creation of spatial forms that unify "the symbolic environment of the elite around the world, thus superseding the historical specificity of each locale" (p. 447). Castells hypothesizes that the *space of flow* will make for the proliferation of an ahistorical and acultural architecture—reflecting the fact that we no longer belong to any place and to any culture. This *architecture of nudity* makes no pretension of conveying any meaning. "Its message is the silence" (p. 450). The spaces and designs that emerge out of the *space of flow* therefore aim to keep us relationally (culturally) suspended by keeping our notions of self, identity, and society anchorless. Still, Castells believes that architecture, because it has the ability to preserve meanings in the generation of knowledge, makes for a good site to resist this coming domination. It also makes for the reconciliation of culture and technology, and, in so doing, allows us to build cultural, political, and physical bridges that stop us from "heading toward life in parallel universes" (Castells, 2002, p. 459).

But within Castells' analysis we find problems that plague other analyses about how emerging technologies will alter our worlds. We still find a deficient understanding of communication—communication is still about transmission. This helps explain why Castells has a striking tendency to downplay the complexity and potentiality of the human component. In fact, the human component is nearly nonexistent in Castells' analyses, making for what Jan van Dijk (2002) interestingly—and quite correctly—refers to as Castells' "one-dimensional network society."

Our social, media, and informational networks will always remain contextually (humanly) embedded (van Dijk, 2002). That is, such networks will always remain connected to a social, physical, psychological, and biological context (van Dijk, 2002). The result being that our social, media, and informational networks will always be shaped and laden with our fears, suspicions, biases, prejudices, hopes, and ambitions. We will therefore never attain, as Castells forecasts, a *real virtuality* that will completely disembody our social relationships. "A realist and hopeful perspective of virtuality is that it adds to organic social life, instead of replacing it, and that it is able to launch all kinds of fruitful interplay between them" (van Dijk, 2002)

But such an interplay first requires that we redefine our understanding of what being human means. Castells' analysis actually fails to appreciate the full human cost that emerging technologies—ontologically premised on notions of separation and fragmentation (duality)—exact on self, identity, and society. Human beings can only tolerate so much separation and fragmentation. If both persist, as Castells' analysis is suggesting—even encouraging—our demise— and all the human misery and destruction that come with our demise—is all but certain. We will ultimately pay a horrendous price for promoting technologies that create spaces and designs that are bent on pushing us towards "different universes" and "different dimensions."

Bringing dialogue to our understanding of space pushes us to adopt a more organic and local conception of space and design. No longer would the design of our spaces be left solely in the hands of architects and planners, or seen merely as a technical activity. Instead of merely addressing issues about aesthetics and functionality, we will now push architects and planners to also wrestle with emancipatory issues. We will also look closer at how emerging technologies are altering our conceptions of space and shaping our interactions with each other, the world, and our own humanity. Dialogue gives us a rigorous calculus to understand the effects of such technologies, as well the means to imagine new and different technologies—ones that will hopefully make for more human-centered futures. It also reminds us to focus always on the contexts from where new technologies are emerging, as all technologies have a social context. In the end, dialogue will always affirm the notion of emergence. It will always be more important *what* processes we use to create our spaces rather than *how* our spaces and designs look and function. As much as we can learn and borrow ideas from Paolo Solerie, Frank Gehry, Charles Jencks, and other architects, designers, and planners who are pursuing new kinds of spaces and designs, we always have to remain true to dialogue and the promise of emergence.

Final Thoughts

In *Supermodernism: Architecture in the Age of Globalization*, Hans Ibelings (1998) writes approvingly about a new architecture that is much different than what Jencks celebrates and anticipates. This new architecture is emerging out of a "new interest in the modernist aesthetic and . . . a revival of the idea that the processes of modernization are the driving force behind architectural and urbanist innovation" (p. 129). It also reflects "a declining interest in accommodating a symbolic cargo or rendering a—sometimes only half-under-stood—philosophical or scientific idea" (p. 129). Moreover, whereas a lot of recent architecture seeks to appeal to the intellect, this new architecture "attaches greater importance to visual, spatial, and tactile sensation" (p. 133).

This evolution excites Ibelings. He believes that supermodernism releases architects from "the compulsive tendency to construe everything in symbolic terms" and "the onerous duty to keep on producing meaningful architecture" (p. 133). "The moralism and dogmatism implicit in postmodernism have made way for realism" (p. 133).

Ibelings' contempt for postmodernism is explicit. He believes that postmodernism is responsible for the general sentiment "that modern architecture has nothing to say" and thus should remain silent. Many persons would no doubt take issue with this claim. Still, this new architecture moves us backward rather forward in our quest for spaces and designs that foreground the human element. Supermodernism inherits all of modernism's ontological, epistemological, and axiological positions. It gives us no new understandings of the human condition. We remain beholden to the view that there is no moral, existential, and spiritual relation between communication and the human condition. Supermodernism, in fact, relegitimizes the status quo in the most vicious of ways by responding to postmodernism rather than modernism's perilous threat to the world. Its emphasis on sensation also blocks any rigorous interrogation of how our spaces and designs bear on the human condition. Sensation, like thought, is by no means ontologically neutral. How we visually, spatially, and tactilely experience our spaces and designs is related to how we perceive and understand our position in the world. Simply put, sensation is an ontological artifact. We still have to deal with what worldviews make for what sensations. So supermodernism's boast of promoting realism and pragmatism is highly suspect. It has, as with any other worldview, its own mysticism.

Ibelings' claim that supermodernism releases architects of the burden of dealing with meaning and symbols in no way alters the fact that our spaces and designs are shot through with ideology and, as a result, will always have implications and consequences for meaning and meaning creation processes. We can never avoid meaning. We would no doubt be better served by looking at what kinds of meanings and meaning creation processes our spaces and designs promote, and the implications and consequences of those meanings and processes on the world and us. Such an approach will help us realize a new architecture that promotes a deep relation to the world and enlarges our understanding of what being human means. We will also find in this new architecture spaces and designs that move in harmony with the quantum rhythms of the world; that promote the evolution of our moral capacity by reminding us of our deep moral, existential, and spiritual connection to the world and each other; that lessen the threat of our differences by encouraging attention to our common humanness and humanity; and, ultimately, that promote communion with the world by making us less afraid of the world and each other.

III

Locating and Dislocating Community in a Global World

Race, ethnicity, nationality, sexual orientation, and other such identity constructs are *really* expressions of spaces. After all, such notions make for the construction of spaces that limit and control our relations and interactions with others. In this way, such spaces act like physical spaces, allowing us to control who has access to our worlds. On the other hand, however, such spaces tend to be categorical and oppositional. We are either Black or White, homosexual or heterosexual, male or female, rich or poor, Christian or Muslim, and so forth. We are spatially discouraged from being ambiguous. Race, ethnicity, and other such constructs tell us what corners of the world we belong to, what are our politics and ethics, and which Gods we must worship.

We commonly define our identity by our differences rather than by our common humanness. We focus on our different spaces rather than our common spaces. We use our race, nationality, and other such constructs to limit ourselves physically, emotionally, existentially, and spiritually. We privilege those relationships that are shaped by physical proximity. Naturally, such relationships tend to be born out of commonality—whether through commonality of language, race, ethnicity, experiences, or being. We believe that such commonality is necessary for order, unity, and the making of the *good society*. In reality, such commonality retards us mentally, emotionally, and spiritually by discouraging us from developing ways of being that foster compassion, trust, and openness and that come with dealing with peoples of different situations and backgrounds.

We can never be without a conception of space or belong to all spaces. Moreover, race, gender, ethnicity, sexual orientation, and nationality will remain integral to how we understand ourselves and, consequently, remain an integral component in how we define space. It is also in the interest of the status quo to keep such notions as the defining rules in the construction of identity. On the other hand, however, the quantum order of the world is constantly undermining the identity stability that comes with race, ethnicity, and other such constructs. That is, the quantum order of the world is significantly altering how we construct identity and, consequently, altering our conception of space. We are increasingly being less defined by race, ethnicity, and so on, and as a result, increasingly resisting the confines of such spaces. But what becomes of our commonly held notions of identity and community in a world where the "distances between global spaces are collapsing, contracting, spreading, fracturing, suturing, unifying, and subducting through developments in social life?" What becomes of our spaces and designs in an increasingly global, plural, and multicultural world that seems bent on undermining homogenous and stable notions of identity and community and the cultural, political, and social institutions that perpetuate these notions? What kinds of spaces and designs would help us lessen the threat of our differences as our distances and spaces collapse, contract, and collide?

Our increasingly global and multicultural world is subtly imposing new conceptions of identity and community on us. These conceptions tend to be highly fluid and expansive and have no origins or obligations to physical spaces. For instance, we are increasingly identifying ourselves as sexual rather heterosexual or homosexual, racial rather than black or white, spiritual rather than religious, as citizens of the world rather than as citizens of any one country, and so on. We now have the challenge of finding new conceptions of community that promote and complement these emergent conceptions of identity.

We need emergent conceptions of community that have the ontological capacity and elasticity to deal with this diversity. On the other hand, the world is also simultaneously witnessing the rise of highly rigid and fundamentalist notions of identity, nearly all of which have origins and deep obligations to various spaces and places. For instance, many commentators warn ominously about the coming clash of civilizations and cultures. Samuel Huntington of Harvard University, for example, contends that "The preservation of the United States and the West requires the renewal of Western identity." Also, Morgan Norval (2002) believes that the West needs to reassert its Christian heritage so as to prevail in its supposed death struggle with the Muslim world.

> To a great extent, the war on terrorism is a clash of civilizations, as Islam is fundamentally anti-Western; thus, the prospects of success are limited. Unless we recognize that we are engaged in the revival of the centuries old clash between Islam and the Christian West and act accordingly, we face a future where the best we can hope for is to keep terrorists acts to a manageable level. If Islam does not self-destruct, it will remain a bitter foe of the West and the forces of globalization, and it will hold to its age-old worldview in which it is at war with the non-Muslim world.

Indeed, the horrendous events of September 11, 2001 did nothing to alleviate our fears and suspicions about the diversity that is emerging out of our increasingly global and multicultural world. We now discursively associate diversity with evil. Yet the course of the world cannot be reversed or stopped. Our distances will continue to collapse, contract, and collide. We have to find community with each other. The only question now is *How*? As Nobel Laureate Amartya Sen (2000) notes, "The central issue here is not how dissimilar the distinct societies may be from one another, but what ability and opportunity the members of one society have—or can develop—to appreciate and understand how others function." There is arguably is no more important issue facing this new millennium.

Searching for Community

I teach a graduate level class entitled *Communication & Community*. The primary objective of this course is to develop emergent understandings of community. We focus on such questions as, *What is community?   Why community?   How do different peoples do community*? We look at many different understandings of community and try to identify the different worldviews, assumptions, and positions that inform different understandings of community. We also look at the different implications that flow from different understandings of community and try to identify the communicative, performative, and rhetorical practices that attend to different understandings of community.

On the first day of the semester I ask each student to articulate her definition of community. Our task is to identify and lay bare all of the discursive forces that constitute our own definition of community. What hopes, fears, assumptions, values, truths, beliefs, biases, prejudices, and life experiences bring us to our own different definitions of community?   What implications and consequences attend to our different understandings of community?   The interrogation is often painfully revealing. I try to keep my students honest. I gently push them to deal with various beliefs, values, and so forth that are being left unaccounted for. I also push them to reckon with *all* of the implications and consequences that attend to their various definitions. Through this pedagogical stance I hope for my students to understand how worldviews constitute us and thereby powerfully shape how we understand and experience the world. I also want them to appreciate how thickly layered we are with all kinds of fears, suspicions, anxieties, values, beliefs, and so forth. Finally, I want them to appreciate the complex nature of this layering and how it insidiously influences the ways we embody and understand the world, each other, and even our own humanity.

Understandably, resistance is the norm for most of my students. Many resist more aggressively than others. One student even jokingly described my interrogation as akin to a blood-letting procedure. Understandably, my students' first reaction is to protect and justify their definitions of community. I understand the vulnerability that comes with doing the work that I am asking them to do, and I empathize continually. Initially, most students are unconvinced that so much "stuff" resides in their definitions of community. It is, after all, only a definition, and one that was written quickly at that. Still, the many different and conflicting definitions of community that soon appear make quite clear that we are all coming to community from different positionalities, and that such different positionalities come with different implications and consequences for how we enter community. I remind my students again and again that our primary goal is to understand and reckon with the implications and consequences of our various understandings of community. We have no interest in morally judging any conception of community. It soon becomes apparent, anyway, that such judging is arbitrary. Ultimately, all that really matters are the implications and consequences that attend to our different understandings of community.

What is particularly striking over the few years that I have been teaching this class is that most students explicitly define community in relation to homogeneity, commonality, and even proximity. Community is a location and destination—a place that we arrive at when we possess the necessary homogeneity or commonality or share the same physical place. In a word, community is a noun. Community is a group in proximity that shares a value set (integrity, morality, faith, loyalty). Community is a place where people co-exist in shared experience. Community is the bond that holds together human beings who may share similar values, beliefs, experiences and norms. A community is a group of beings unified by one or more common factors, such as language, traditions, nationality, ideology, religion, area of residence, etc. Community is a group of people joined together by language, rituals, and geography. Community is a group of individuals who live in close proximity to each other as well as depend on one another for either social, financial, or spiritual purposes. Community is a group of people sharing a commonality of some kind, and working together to achieve common goals, standards, values, and so forth. Community consists of people sharing some element of commonality. Community is a feeling of belonging to a group of people because of a commonality shared between the members; whether it be where they live, shared hobbies, etc. Community is a sense of cohesiveness between a group of people that may be based on location, beliefs, values or other commonalities in their identities.

As our discussions evolve in the classroom, we soon realize that diversity emerges as a threat to any conception of community where homogeneity or commonality is the defining element. All of the definitions of community that privilege homogeneity assume that too much diversity, or the wrong kinds of diversity, ultimately undermine the homogeneity and commonality necessary for community. As such, we tend to assume that community requires constant protection from diversity—which is also to say that diversity commands a certain amount of suspicion and surveillance from us. Whereas diversity probably enhances and flavors community life, we assume that homogeneity ultimately constitutes and sustains it.

Of course, my students profess a deep commitment to diversity, and they are often wearing the political buttons, to boot. Still, they are uncomfortable with the unconscious privileging of homogeneity that is emerging in their definitions of community. When pressed, however, they admit that certain diverse practices and arrangements simply have to be discouraged, even censored, even prosecuted. After all, what modern community can tolerate, say, gender, race, and sexual discrimination? However, my students are uncertain about what framework should be employed to distinguish appropriate from inappropriate practices and arrangements. We discuss the perils and problems of different frameworks. We discuss the admissions of Stanley Fish, Michael Walzer, and other prominent proponents of toleration, who write that toleration comes with a host of intractable moral and theoretical problems. In the end, my students' conceptions of community frustrate them.

But why do so many of us casually assume that homogeneity or commonality or proximity needs to be the defining element of our conceptions of community? What is the worldview origin and location of this assumption? What are the implications and consequences of this assumption for community and the world, especially a world where our distances and spaces are collapsing and colliding? What is the veracity of this assumption? In other words, what are the worldview origins of our deep fear and suspicion of diversity? What about this fear that tends to grip us so deeply?

Our common conceptions of community are unredeemable in this emergent global and multicultural world. The diversity that promises to emerge from this world—from our distances and spaces collapsing, contracting, and fracturing— is simply too much for our common conceptions of diversity to bear. We never could have anticipated this much diversity. Our dominant worldview is born out of a less turbulent period and thereby simply assumes that homogeneity and stability are—and need to be—the order of the world. Thus, as we confront this increasingly diverse world, or as this increasingly diverse world confronts us, we still assume that the challenge we face is to find ways of processing this diversity so as to ensure that we possess the homogeneity necessary for civility and progress. For instance, Ira Katznelson (2002) of Columbia University contends that liberalism's most basic, current conundrum resides in "how to broaden its endowments in order to protect and nourish heterogeneity while coping with its perils" (p. 10). Peter Salins of Hunter College of the City University of New York argues for an emergent assimilation politics that rests on four pillars: (a) adherence to everything that the U.S. Constitution espouses, (b) promotion of a commitment to market capitalism, (c) the embracing of the density and redundancy of institutional life, and (d) the fostering of a commitment to modernity and progress that permeates all U.S. society. He believes that assimilation is at the foundation of the United States' unsurpassed prosperity, social cohesion, and overall superior evolution. He is, therefore, surprised that many persons would even dream of tinkering with a process that has made for our "greatness." In fact, Salins is appalled:

> How could America's intellectual and political leaders be so short-sighted as to cast away thoughtlessly the paradigm of assimilation that had proved invaluable in unifying the nation for over a century and a half? . . . . The history of the past thirty years has shown that America's opinion and policy elites made a terrible mistake by turning away from assimilation and negating the assimilation contract. And it has, indeed, been the country's leaders—the media, in education, in government, and in corporate America—who have been specifically responsible. The rank and file of ordinary Americans were never consulted, and if they had been, they would have rejected the abandonment of the assimilation paradigm. But regardless of where the fault lies, if ever there was a time to promote assimilation, it is today. . . . The United States' two-hundred year history of maintaining national unity while accommodating ethnic diversity may be robust enough to withstand a temporary defection from the ethos and practice of assimilation, but it cannot withstand it for long before a host of unhappy consequences is unleashed. (pp. 15-16)

Salins believes that our abandonment of an assimilation politics in the U.S. threatens disunity, devolution, and chaos.

> In the end, though, the greatest danger looming for the United States is inter-ethnic conflict, the scourge of almost all other nations with ethnically diverse populations. Assimilation has been our country's secret weapon in diffusing such conflict before it occurs, and without a strong assimilationist ethos, we leave ourselves open for such misfortune. Assimilation is not really about people of different racial, religious, linguistic, or cultural backgrounds becoming alike; it is about people of different . . . backgrounds believing they are irrevocably part of the same national family. It is this belief that allows them to transcend their narrow ethnic loyalties and that blunts, to the point of insignificance, the spurs of ethnic conflict and discord. (p. 17)

But this is exactly the point. We do nothing but tinker. Katznelson's enlightened liberalism and Salins' emergent assimilation politics represent nothing but tinkering. Neither engages in any interrogation of the ontological positions that constitute our dominant paradigm. We all assume that diversity inherently threatens disunity and chaos. We are therefore all searching for the machinery—whether liberalism, global capitalism, fundamentalism, and so forth—that is powerful enough to process the diversity now upon us. We all assume that with a powerful enough machinery we can neutralize this diversity and thereby stop disunity and chaos.

But we are under-appreciating the amount and the kind of diversity that is upon us. There is no machinery that can process this diversity. Diversity is ontological rather than cultural. In other words, diversity has always been, and will always remain, the order of the world. It is the measure of all organic systems. Such systems flourish by promoting diversity and, conversely, perish when they lose diversity. Diversity is therefore a hallmark feature of life.

Our increasingly global, plural, and multicultural world requires emergent conceptions of community that begin with the premise of diversity rather than homogeneity. We need a worldview that actually celebrates diversity—one that gives us an ethics and politics that promote the evolution of new and different ways of experiencing the world. Such a worldview will also promote new kinds of spaces and designs—spaces and designs that pull us towards each other and thereby make us more public and less private. Indeed, an increasingly global, plural, and multicultural world requires spaces and designs that promote relationships rather than contacts, communication rather than interaction, community rather than networks. But as much as our global spaces are increasingly collapsing and contracting, our spaces, as seen in the rise of gated communities and hyper-suburbs, are also simultaneously fragmenting and balkanizing. No doubt, this trend needs to concern us. These spaces and designs will only help to further mystify us and thereby heighten our suspicion of each other's differences. As much as contact, or the possibility of contact, has no direct relation to the promotion of diversity, *no* contact cannot be seen as a plus in an increasingly multicultural world. On the other hand, our spaces and designs are foremost reflective—reflecting and revealing our deepest fears, suspicions, prejudices, values, assumptions, and beliefs. We can therefore only end the fragmentation in our spaces and designs by moving towards a worldview that releases us of all the forces that promote fragmentation.

Community as a Verb

My students will often insist that we suffer together. They want to know my definition of community. I say that *community is about our questing for communion.* Then the interrogation gleefully begins: What do you mean by questing? What do you mean by communion? I answer that questing reflects a striving that comes out of the center of our being, and communion is about our transcending our physical, personal, and primal selves. I share Erich Fromm's claim that human beings possess a striving for union. In *The Art of Loving*, Fromm (1956) writes, "This desire for interpersonal fusion is the most powerful striving in man. It is the most fundamental passion, it is the force which keeps the human race together, the clan, the family, society. The failure to achieve it means insanity or destruction—self-destruction of others" (p. 17). In other words, through union we become human by enlarging our capacity to love.

Human separation reflects human relations that disconnect us from each other through fear, distrust, suspicion, and apathy. Such relations, according to Fromm, make us less human, less decent, less civil, and less moral by undercutting our capacity for love and compassion. Ultimately, such relations foster alienation—alienation from each other and our own humanity. Fromm (1973) contends that alienation makes for powerlessness. It undermines our ability to act purposefully and courageously upon the world. Fromm thus gives us a means to understand suburban and hyper-suburban electoral voting trends, such as the increasing hostility and apathy of suburbanites and hyper-suburbanites to urban problems, and to understand the increasing fragmentation and alienation being found within suburban and hyper-suburban enclaves and gated communities (e.g., Blakely & Snyder, 1999; Bullard, Grigsby & Lee, 1994; Cutler, Glaeser, & Vigdor, 1999; Putnam, 2000).

Community is about us moving from the personal to the relational and, in so doing, recognizing our embeddedness and connectedness to the world and to each other. We *are* a relationship with the world and each other. Community is also about us contesting the forces, practices, and arrangements that sustain the illusion that our interests and well-being are separate from others' interests and well-being. The challenge of community is moving towards a humanity that dialectically embraces both diversity and homogeneity. As Ronald Arnett (1986) notes, "An invitation to human community needs to permit and encourage the emergence of human uniqueness." Such diversity emerges only through an unequivocal commitment to dialogue.

Many factors, arrangements, and practices undermine our questing for communion. One factor is simply the lack of courage—our own unwillingness to risk life. There are also political, social, and cultural arrangements that promote individualism, classism, nationalism, regionalism, and other obstacles to communion that appeal to our primal instincts and impulses. Such arrangements promote a deep distrust and suspicion of the human condition. We come to assume that we have no inherent striving and capacity for communion, and no moral, existential, and spiritual capacity to build communities that reflect the highest expressions of selflessness and compassion. In my students' many definitions of community I find no such conceptions of community. I also find no conceptions of community that assume any moral, existential, and spiritual origin of community. The conceptions of community that I consistently find make no demands on us. There are no moral, existential, and spiritual demands on us to love more, care more, empathize more, imagine more, give more, tolerate more, and so forth. In most cases, the origins of my students' conceptions of community reside in necessity and utility.

Indeed, cheap conceptions of community are common. Community merely demands some element of commonality or homogeneity or proximity. In the case of a gated community, for example, community merely demands that we have sufficient resources to afford a house in a certain location. But any community that demands cheap admission also allows for easy exiting; which is to say that such a community, in demanding nothing much from us, offers no bonds of deep commitment. For instance, residents of gated communities consistently report high levels of isolation and the absence of any *real* community. In my students' conceptions of community I find a deep suspicion and fear of the human condition. I am in no way surprised. For I also deeply possess this fear and suspicion. Our social, cultural, and political systems have properly instilled this fear in all of us. I therefore understand only too well why my students hold to cheap conceptions of community.

But cheap conceptions of community do nothing for us. In fact, such conceptions harm us. As Robert Putnam (2000) compellingly concludes, the U.S. is in the throes of a perilous crisis of community, and the human fallout is proving to be catastrophic. About the relationship between community and being human, Putnam notes, "Dozens of painstaking studies have established beyond reasonable doubt that social connectedness is one of the most powerful determinants of our well-being. The more integrated we are with our community, the less likely we are to experience colds, heart attacks, strokes, cancer, depression, and premature deaths of all sorts" (p. 326). Of course in no way do *all* of our communities need to fulfill *all* of our needs and strivings. What matters is our ability to construct and sustain those communities that we ultimately need, as human beings, to prosper. However, Putnam's findings show plainly that we are without even these vital communities. This reality should in no way surprise us. Any worldview that promotes a deep distrust and suspicion of our humanity puts us at odds with any decent conception of community. How can we be selfless and open in the face of such distrust and suspicion?

The Promise of Community

We need emergent conceptions of community that are capable of fostering levels of bonding among the diverse peoples who are increasingly sharing our spaces and places. Such communities implicate a whole new way of understanding, experiencing, and embodying the world. Moreover, such communities implicate new spaces and designs. Looking at community in terms of communion gives us one such conception of community, but pushing forward this definition will be difficult because it demands so much of us and, more problematically, because homogeneity remains discursively hegemonic. Also, as we continue to define community in terms of homogeneity, we will insist on conceptions of communities that stress proximity.

Katznelson believes that *only* liberalism, with its commitment to citizenship, civil society, human rights, equality before the law, popular sovereignty, social justice, and scientific rationality, is capable of dealing with the world's increasing heterogeneity. In fact, Katznelson believes that in the aftermath of the horrendous events of September 11, 2001 we need to assert an enlightened political liberalism, one that boldly espouses a universal set of categories and concepts. He contends that a "rote defense of liberalism could very well authorize a new brand of colonialism, once again making many non-Western peoples ineligible for its core values of rights, toleration, participation, and consent" (p. 7). However, Katznelson acknowledges a deep paradox, "The global appeal of an enlightened liberalism cannot help but jeopardize the local attachments, the historical particularities—the human plurality—that constitutes its most important rationale" (p. 10). In short, Katznelson believes we must be ready to sacrifice diversity so that we can attain the civility and progress that will come from the homogeneity that liberalism will presumably provide.

Dipesh Chakrabarty, who Katznelson quotes approvingly, contends that liberalism's universal categories and concepts have "historically provided a strong foundation on which to erect—both in Europe and outside—critiques of socially unjust practices. . . .This heritage is now global" (p. 9). But one can only wonder what Chakrabarty thinks of Gertrude Himmelfarb's famous claim that ideas of "justice," "right," "reason," and "love of humanity" are "predominantly, perhaps even uniquely, Western values." Still, Katznelson believes that liberalism's foundational premises will always prevail.

> Both liberalism and the Enlightenment within which it nestles advances a philosophical anthropology of rational actors and rational action, insisting that human agents develop the capacity to deliberate, choose, and achieve sensible goals. In their effort to cultivate such rational citizens, liberal regimes in the past have all too often imposed various limits, drawing boundaries that stunt the capacities of individuals based on their religion, race, gender, literacy, criminality, or colonized status. But after centuries of struggle about the dimensions of freedom, enlightened political liberalism today acknowledges no legitimate barriers to reason, hence no legitimate ascriptive barriers to liberal inclusion and liberal citizenship. (p. 9-10)

So the making of the good society requires that we act rationally and promote rational action. The suggestion here, of course, is that diversity orbits in the realm of non-rational action. Conversely, we behave properly and sensibly when we behave rationally. But rationality is always culturally defined. In fact, rationality, as seen through the prism of liberalism, is a myth. We are rational, as well as cultural, sensual, emotional, social, relational, historical, and existential beings. We are infinitely complex, and no action or decision escapes this complexity. As such, in promoting the notion of rational (acultural) action, liberalism perpetuates a shallow and overly-narrow understanding of human action and, by that, the human condition. Moreover, in elevating the notion of rational action, liberalism promotes a deep distrust and suspicion of our sensual, spiritual, emotional, relational, historical, and cultural selves. It discourages us from embracing, much less celebrating, our full humanity, with all its complexity, ambiguity, and—yes—mystery. The result being that liberalism gives us an overly-narrow view of the world and proposes overly-narrow solutions to our problems.

Katznelson's championing of liberalism makes believe that only we in the Western world believe in supposedly rational action (acting civilly and sensibly). Rationality is supposedly our hallmark contribution to the world, along with the scientific rationality that is born out of it. Katznelson also makes believe that only we in the Western world engage in rational action, which is to say that our actions and institutions are inherently morally superior. For instance, we believe that only we can possess weapons of mass destruction. Supposedly, only we can be trusted to use these weapons rationally. Also, the promotion of liberalism suggests that other civilizations are somehow deficient in the social, cultural, and political apparatuses that stress and promote rational action. The peoples of such civilizations therefore have no moral ground to question our actions and decision. We are inherently decent and civil because our actions are supposedly rational.

But what is civil about our unrelenting destruction and plundering of the world's ecosystems and natural resources? What is civil about our promotion of consumerism and materialism? What is civil about the criminalization of various herbs? On the other hand, what is non-rational and uncivil about ancient philosophical systems like Jainism, Gnosticism, Hinduism, and Buddhism that stress love, compassion, mercy, and living in harmony with the natural world? What about liberalism that is morally and politically superior to these philosophical systems? What is deficient about these systems that makes *only* liberalism vital for our prosperity? When exactly did these systems stop giving us a "strong foundation on which to erect . . . critiques of socially unjust practices?" Evidently, what is at work here, as Amartya Sen (2000) explains, is nothing other than Western dominance:

> One consequence of Western dominance of the world today is that other cultures and traditions are often identified and defined by their contrasts with contemporary Western culture. Different cultures are thus interpreted in ways that reinforce the political conviction that Western civilization is somehow the main, perhaps the only, source of rationalistic and liberal ideas—among them analytical scrutiny, open debate, political tolerance, and agreement to differ. The West is seen, in effect, as having exclusive access to the values that lie at the foundation of rationality and reasoning, science and evidence, liberty and tolerance, and of course rights and justice.

Katznelson contends that the making of the good society resides in liberalism's promotion of a set of universal practices and concepts. But what makes love, compassion, and mercy less capable of dealing with the world's increasing diversity? What concepts are more universal? We are to believe that these concepts lack the necessary durability and rigidity to deal with this diversity and the supposed imperfectability of human nature that makes for what Hannah Arendt labels "radical evil." Presumably, only liberalism can deal with these tough realities.

> A wholesale rejection of enlightened liberalism as a mere figment of Western imperialism could very well license an irresponsible and foundationless anti-modernism, reinforcing a mirror-image view of 'us' against 'them.' Intransigently advanced, each perspective evades asking how we can shade the sensibilities, deepen the capacities, and address the limitations of the liberal tradition in full awareness that credulous notions of human perfectibility have

been mocked by the global diffusion of human superfluousness. (Katznelson, 2002, p. 7)

We therefore need liberalism because we are inherently imperfect, and liberalism will always have limitations and imperfections because we are, again, inherently imperfect. Liberalism is simply the best that can be had. But no reasoning can be more dangerously naïve and overly simplistic. Human perfection is a bogeyman. Yet it works, in the case of liberalism, by discouraging us from seeking more complex understandings of the human condition; which is to say that it blocks any deep interrogation of our own humanity. It thereby works to legitimize arrangements that demand less from us—arrangements that put no onus on us to love more, to care more, to give more, to empathize more, and so forth. The notion of human imperfection works to release us from the condition of the world. Now we merely have to look to the gods and the heavens for our redemption, or simply accept the nihilism that comes with a secular world.

I am in no way denying that human beings are inherently imperfect. Just the same, I am in no way contending that human beings are inherently perfect. In my view, both positions are simplistic and nonheuristic. Human perfection, after all, is a non-issue in the world's dominant spiritual teachings. In these teachings, redemption is consistently framed in terms of what we do rather than what we are. I believe that the notion of *completion* is a much more heuristic way of constructing our discourse of the human condition. Completion assumes that we have the ability and capacity to be better human beings. We can care more, love more, give more, empathize more, imagine more, and so forth. How much more we can possibly be we will never really know. What really matters is that we can be better human beings and thereby make a more just and humane world. As such, completion pushes us to look more holistically at the human condition. It also emphasizes action over abstraction by encouraging us to look at our own potential, rather than in abstract institutions, to make new and better worlds. We would ultimately hold ourselves to higher levels of accountability by claiming more responsibility for our actions and inactions. We would no longer view community as a noun, as something we can stumble into because of something we arbitrarily possess or share. In short, completion encourages a more proactive and generative conception of community.

Final Thoughts

Various prophets teach that God calls us to establish community rather than religion. Never was there a time when this call was more pertinent and the stakes more perilous. In fact, the world now seems increasingly determined to force us to find community by organically collapsing and contracting the distances between us. It also seems just as determined to push us towards richer understandings of community and, in so doing, demanding that we move beyond extant understandings of the world. We could, of course, continue to resist this work, but our actions and inactions come at a perilous price.

We could also continue to believe that we can somehow neutralize and subdue the world's diversity. We are entitled to our futility, though such futility will come at a cost. But to assume that our redemption resides in community is to adopt a different stance to the world. Whereas on one hand we can look at our collapsing and contracting spaces and distances with fear and dread, on the other we can look at this trend in terms of hope and anticipation. An increasingly global and multicultural world is richly laden with infinite new realities and possibilities. No world is more fecund, and no world pushes us more to enlarge our humanity by demanding that we care more, give more, imagine more, and so on. Our emergent world thus possesses the capacity to be a blessed world.

IV

Searching for New Spaces in Spanglish

We are increasingly bending and stretching identity in ways and at speeds that the world has probably never seen before. "Movement is [indeed] status quo," and the movement that Ed Morales (2002) is referring to in *Living in Spanglish: The search for Latino identity in America* is what many Latinos throughout the U.S. are fondly calling Spanglish.

> At the root of Spanglish is a very universal state of being. It is a displacement from one place, home, to another place, home, in which one feels at home in both places, yet at home in neither place. It is a kind of banging-one's-head-against-the-wall state, and the only choice you have left is to embrace the transitory (read transnational) state of in-between. (Morales, 2002, p. 7)

Spanglish is a "forward-looking race that obliterates all races" by embracing all races. It is "a call to end race" as we commonly understand race. "But in order to face down race, we must first immerse ourselves in it. In all of them" (Morales, 2002, p. 14). Moreover, Spanglish is "a space where multiple levels of identification is possible" (Morales, 2002, p. 17); akin, Morales believes, to what Michel Foucault calls a heterotopic space—"a kind of effectively enacted utopia in which all the other real sites that can be found within the culture are simultaneously represented, contested, and inverted" (quoted in Morales, 2002, p. 17). Spanglish is also akin to what Pico Iyer (2000) describes in *The Global Soul: Jet lag, shopping malls, and the search for home* as the global soul—a person who "has grown up in many cultures all at once—and so lived in the cracks between them" (p. 18).

Spanglish is therefore more than a long-term racial miscegenation process occurring among Latinos in the U.S., and definitely more than the evolution of a language that fuses English and Spanish. It is, in fact, about the evolution of an identity that is finally disconnected—liberated, really—from one race, one place, one space, one language, one vision, one history, and so on. As such, "there is no prescribed form, no cultural norms involved in being Spanglish—

the world of Spanglish is the world of the multiracial individual" (Morales, 2002, p. 9). It is the culture of the future because it has no score to settle with the past. More importantly, Spanglish is simply—and finally—about more and more persons recognizing that the future will always afford more possibilities than the past. It represents the triumph of heterogeneity, multisubjectivity, and multiplicity, and celebrates a "permanently evolving, and rapidly expanding difference" (Morales, 2002, p. 26). In this way, Spanglish is about the end of culture—and race and ethnicity—as a noun. It is about *culturing*. In other words, Spanglish demonstrates that no culture, no race, no ethnicity, no language, is inherently stable and homogenous.

Intercultural and post-colonial scholars are more and more writing about *placing* and *racing* and *differencing*—instead of ethnicity and race and difference—so as to afford a more heuristic understanding of the complexity, discontinuity, and diversity that constitute race, ethnicity, and difference (Dervin, 1991; Fry, 1998; Olmsted, 1998; Rodriguez, 2002a, Said, 2000). Indeed, verbing our understanding of culture allows us to see the many points of conflict, dissent, and diversity that characterize all cultures (Belay, 1993; Casmir, 1993; Chen & Starosta, 1996; Dervin, 1991; Martin & Nakayama, 1999; McPhail, 1996; Rodriguez, 2002a; Said, 2000; Shutter, 1993; Starosta, 1991).

Cultures are constantly negotiating the interplay between ambiguity and meaning, chaos and order, homogeneity and diversity, equilibrium and disequilibrium, agency and structure, and other such quantum and dialectical tensions (Rodriguez, 2002a). The result being that cultures are always in flux; that is, always reckoning with instability and change (Martin & Nakayama, 1999; Rodriguez, 2002a). Masking this flux exaggerates (and distorts) our perceptions of homogeneity and stability, forcing us to adopt dichotomous stances that stop us from "moving toward multiple perspectives that might inform each other in a dialogue of differences" (Dervin, 1991, p. 50). Culturing attempts to meet our needs for more complex understandings of how we constitute cultures, so as to speak better to the complexity, discontinuity, and diversity that all cultures inherently possess and to help us devise means to have more constructive and nonviolent ways to deal with our rich and infinite differences. It reflects our proclivity to construct new and different meanings, understandings, and practices, so as to reckon with the world's infinite ambiguity and quantum nature that constantly destabilize extant meanings, understandings, and practices. As such, the spaces that different cultures, races, and ethnicities claim as a birthright are inherently permeable and heterogeneous.

Culturing is born out of our uniquely human need to bring meaning to bear upon the world's ambiguity. It represents the various tensions and rhythms that come with our trying to find and hold onto meanings in a world that is inherently quantum in consciousness. It answers the call for "a way to acknowledge and accept those aspects of dialectical inquiry that contribute to self-reflection and the appreciation of Otherness, and at the same time cultivate an awareness of those aspects that perpetuate symbolic violence" (McPhail, 1996, p. 150). It also gives us a theoretical and political way "to step back from the imaginary thresholds that separate people from each other" by releasing us from the dichotomous labels, spaces, and positionalities that come with such thresholds. Spanglish therefore represents an evolution in race, ethnicity, and culture that is vital for our survival and prosperity in this new millennium.

A world laden with nuclear and other weapons of mass destruction can no longer afford conflict and strife between peoples that construct identity through a purely physical conception of space. Thus, in disconnecting identity from space, Spanglish finally allows us to imagine a world devoid of such conflict and strife. This is arguably a hallmark moment in human history. It represents a moment that most of us could have never imagined. That is, Spanglish speaks to a potentiality most of us felt that human beings never had. We have long made believe that deadly ethnic and racial strife is simply inevitable because of our supposed savage nature. But Spanglish releases us from this belief. Even though ethnic and racial strife will long continue to be with us, Spanglish reveals to us that such strife is in no way inevitable, and thus we are in no way damned to this inevitability. In releasing identity from space, Spanglish allows us to imagine more expansive and inclusive models of identity, and, thereby, more expansive and inclusive models of space. As such, releasing identity from a fixed space, as is commonly believed, in no way weakens identity. In fact, the opposite is true. Identity too, as with other any other organic system, must change and evolve to survive and prosper, and such change is only possible if our models of identity remain fluid and permeable. This is exactly what Spanglish is about. It represents the fullest expression of identity in terms of social evolution.

Spanglish cuts identity loose from physicality and, in so doing, interrupts our organization of human beings by various physical attributes. In other words, Spanglish undermines our use of physical attributes to spatially organize our societies so as to maintain order and social control. But how do we organize our societies when such physical differentiation is no longer possible? This is the challenge that Spanglish is increasingly posing to us. In ending race and ethnicity, Spanglish moves identity from the realm of the primal to that of the spiritual. For instance, in belonging to no one race, we now belong to every race. Spanglish tramples borders, thereby making us increasingly global souls. It frees us from the rigid confines of one race, one ethnicity, one language, one geography, one people, one culture, one history, one reality, one worldview, one god. Such confines only serve to distort and limit what we can become. Spanglish destabilizes how we discursively and spatially organize our worlds. The evolution of Spanglish means that more and more persons are refusing to be confined to one race, one ethnicity, one culture, and so forth. We will no longer allow history to dictate who and what we are, and to whom we will belong to and who will belong to us. This hegemony is just about over, and probably no one understood this better than Eddie Figueroa, a New York conceptual artist, who Ed Morales discusses in *Living in Spanglish*.

Morales (2002) writes that Figueroa was thoroughly obsessed with Latinos being a "multicultural people and that there was no space for us in the conventional world, and we had to invent an imaginary space to allow us to gel" (p. 90). He believed this space could be found in the concept of the Puerto Rican Embassy, which evolved later into the Spirit Republic of Greater Puerto Rico. According to Figueroa,

> The Puerto Rican Embassy is a concept, it's an idea, it's not a physical loca-
> tion. . . . We are dealing with concepts that are beyond geography, beyond three
> dimensions. With the Puerto Rican Embassy, we're declaring our independ-
> ence. The spirit republic is a free place. To win this fight we don't need
> weapons, this is the weapon that's going to win [points to heart]. The
> revolution is here, man. (quoted in Morales, 2002, p. 91).

As Morales (2002) acknowledges, Figueroa did indeed make "it a little easier for Puerto Ricans to be several people at once, in several places, looking backward from the future into the past....It is an idea that is no longer as bizarre as it seemed" (p. 92).

Check Miscellaneous

In *The Global Soul: Jet lag, shopping malls, and the search for home*, Pico Iyer (2000) wonders about whether there is a migratory striving that is making us global souls. He quotes Simone Weil ("We must take the feeling of being at home into exile. We must be rooted in the absence of place."), Thomas Paine ("My country is the world, and my religion is to do good."), and Ralph Waldo Emerson ("What is man but a congress of nations?"). He seems uncertain as to what to make, exactly, of this global soul phenomenon. On one hand, Iyer (2000) believes that "our shrinking world gave more and more of us the chance to see, in palpable, unanswerable ways, how much we [have] in common, and how much we could live . . . beyond petty allegiances and labels, out-side the reach of nation-states" (p. 17). He also writes, "I have grown up, too, with a keen sense of the blessings of being unaffiliated, it has meant that almost everywhere is new and strange to me (as I am new and strange to it), and nearly everywhere allows me to keep alive a sense of wonder and detachment" (Iyer, 2000, p. 24). On the other hand, Iyer (2000) fears that "A lack of affiliation may mean a lack of accountability, and forming a sense of commitment can be hard without a sense of community" (p. 25). Moreover, "Displacement can encourage the wrong kinds of distance, and if the nationalism we see sparking up around the globe arises from a too narrow and fixed sense of loyalty, the international-ism that's coming to birth may reflect a too roaming and undefined sense of belonging" (Iyer, 2000, p. 25). Further, "The Global Soul may see so many sides of every question that he never settles on a firm conviction; he may grow so used to giving back a different self according to his environment that he loses sight of who he is when nobody's around" (Iyer, 2000, p. 25). Yet Iyer (2000) uses the phrase global *soul*, never global citizen, global people, or even global being. He never explains why he uses the word soul, but I believe it speaks to how he experiences his own being in the world, his own evolution from the primal to the spiritual. This is the phrase I would have used. No other phrase better captures my own transcending of race, ethnicity, nationality, and geography.

I too am a global soul. I too am Spanglish. I too am Brown. I too am a Nowherian. I too live between home and exile. I too feel like a congress of nations dwells within me. I too struggle to break free from the confines of one race, one gender, one sexuality, one nationality, one ethnicity, one geography. I too am against the tyranny of borders. I too feel like the half-English, half-Japanese, Malaysian man who says to Iyer, "One country is not enough" (quoted in Iyer, 2000, p. 18). But I would also add: *"One race is not enough." "One ethnicity is not enough." "One culture is not enough." "One cosmology is not enough." "One religion is not enough." "One language is not enough." "One sexuality is not enough."*

> *We feel surrounded, that's the thing. Our borders do not hold. National borders do not hold. Ethnic borders. Religious borders. Aesthetics borders, certainly. Sexual borders. Allergenic borders. We live in the "Age of diversity," in a city of diversity—I do, anyway—so we see what we do not necessarily choose to see: People listing according to internal weathers. We hear what we do not want to hear: Confessions we refuse to absolve. (p. 213)*

> Richard Rodriguez, *Brown: The Last Discovery of America*

Iyer wonders whether we have a migratory impulse. We have, after all, always been moving from place to place. We have never remained confined to one place or space. Movement is status quo. Iyer, however, under-appreciates the movement that is occurring. It is in no way purely migratory. It is much more than people having multiple passports, living in airports, and traveling all over the planet like desperate cultural, racial, and ethnic nomads. In my view, the global soul, as in Spanglish, represents the highest evolutionary point so far achieved or imagined in human history. In fact, the global soul represents the end of history and the coming of a new world—one that ends long-held beliefs, values, truths, and norms. Nothing will no longer be the same.

Inevitably, the question will arise from someone: "Who am I?" which translates to *really* mean "Where are you originally from?" "What is your race?" "Which box do you check off?" "What exactly is your ethnicity?" "What is your first language?" "Did I pronounce your name correctly?" "Where is your accent from?" "Do you miss home?". I never want to answer any of these questions. I want to rebel. Why does it matter, for instance, where I am from? Or what is my race or ethnicity? But in no way do I want to suggest that I am one of those persons who is simply trying to be raceless and spaceless so as to avoid the hassles and responsibilities that come with race and ethnicity. I embrace race and own the history of all races. In wanting to avoid answering these questions, I am identifying with all of the world's oppressed peoples—regardless of race, ethnicity, gender, religion, sexual orientation, or nationality. Still, I believe that answering these questions helps perpetuate a hegemony and world order that I wish to help destroy—the very one that attempts to disconnect my well-being from the poverty stricken people in some ghetto in, say, Brazil. Moreover, these questions have nothing to do with what I am about and the life that I am desperately trying to embody. I really do want to undermine the social ordering and control that commonly-held notions of identity help to perpetuate. But I have grown into this politics.

There were never any boxes for me. There was always one problem or the other. For instance, although I am a U.S. citizen, I was born elsewhere; and although racially I check Black, my father is White and my mother is Black; and so forth. The problem continues to this day. Just recently, one person said fondly to me that he put me under "Miscellaneous." (This time my pedagogical and political stances were responsible for the confusion.) He assured me that it was quite a big box and he was certain I would fit there. Of course miscellaneous really means illegitimate. In many ways this is what I am and what I wish to be. I want to be illegitimate. I want never to be easily categorized, for to be categorized is to say this is what I am, and this subtly bounds me to the present. I wish to belong to the future. I want my illegitimacy to disrupt the dominant order, to push us to ask questions we never once thought of asking, to challenge us to explore realities that seem impossible, to invite us to imagine worlds that seem unimaginable, and to remind to us ask why words like Spanglish get spelling error messages. But when I am formally categorized by others as Miscellaneous, or must simply check the box marked Other, as big as the box probably is, I have to resist because to do otherwise is to facilitate my own marginalization and help sustain the legitimacy of a network of power relations that I believe is only harming the world. In other words, in refusing to be boxed, I am saying that this world is fecundly laden with the potential for other realities and possibilities, and many of these realities and possibilities may never be boxable. I am also saying that the no human institution has any inherent moral authority to box anyone.

But what, exactly, about the boxes given to us as the norm is so legitimate? What about, even, the need to box people like fruit and vegetables? The congress of nations that dwells within me will never allow me to be easily boxed. This is one way I understand Spanglish. It represents the rise of Miscellaneous and the end of categorization. It is about a way of being that defies the concepts and precepts that sustain the status quo. It is about the end of exclusion and separation and the rise of our own evolutionary impulse to defy the forces and practices that impede our social evolution and liberation. So I believe that our impulse to move from one space to the next is really an evolutionary striving, and practices that impede this striving ultimately undermine our prosperity and survival. Thus, unlike Iyer, I have no doubts or suspicions about the coming of the global soul. In fact, I embody and anticipate its coming.

Spanglish and Its Critics

I have no illusions about the coming of the global soul and the rise of Spanglish. However, I also understand the seduction of cooptation. I know the status quo really wants global consumers rather than global souls. I have fears about Spanglish being reduced to merely a language. I also fear this language acquiring all the trappings of a language of power—one that colonizes and assimilates minority languages. I also know that evolution and destruction are dialectically intertwined, and, for this reason, evolution causes us much anxiety. I therefore understand the harsh criticisms Spanglish is catching from Latinos, especially from the Latino intelligentsia. For example, Nobel Laureate Octavio Paz describes Spanglish as an abomination: "Ni es bueno ni es malo, sino abominable" (quoted in Stavans, 2000a, p. 555). And besides finding Spanglish offensive, Roberto Gonzalez Echevarria (1997), Sterling Professor of Hispanic and Comparative Literature at Yale University, believes that "it is naïve to think that we [U.S. Latinos] could create a new language that would be as functional and culturally rich" as Spanish. He believes that Spanglish "poses a grave danger to Hispanic culture and to the advancement of Hispanics in mainstream America" (Gonzalez Echevarria, 1997, p. A.29). "Spanglish is an invasion of Spanish by English" (Gonzalez Echevarria, 1997, p. A.29). Gonzalez Echevarria (1997) also believes "that people should learn languages well and that learning English should be the priority for Hispanics, if they aspire, as they should, to influential positions" (p. A.29). Those who practice Spanglish "are doomed to writing not a minority literature but a minor literature." Indeed, Gonzalez Echevarria makes no apologies for believing that "Spanish is our strongest bond, and it is vital that we preserve it" (p. A.29). Likewise, Antonio Garrido, director of the Instituto Cervantes in New York, an organization created by the Spanish government to promote Spanish and Hispanic-American language and culture, believes that Latinos should strive for good English and good Spanish so as "to have a future" in the United States. "Spanglish has no future" (quoted in Kong, 2003).

I understand why Spanglish's critics believe the sky is about to fall. The nature of the criticisms should in no way surprise us. We have seen these criticisms again and again. Just recently, in fact, we saw Ebonics take the same kind of beating from the African American intelligentsia. In defense of Spanglish, Illan Stavans (2000b) recounts, for example, that Yiddish was never a unified tongue, but rather a series of regional varieties drawn from Hebrew, German, Russian, and other Slavic languages. In fact, such was the contempt for Yiddish that rabbis and the Jewish intelligentsia saw Yiddish as unworthy for biblical dialogue. In 1978, however, the Yiddish author Isaac Bashevis Singer was awarded the Nobel Prize in Literature. As for Spanglish, Richard Rodriguez (2002) writes:

> *Nativists who want to declare English the official language of the United States do not understand the omnivorous appetite of the language they wish to protect. Neither do they understand that their protection would harm our tongue. . . . Those Americans who would build a fence around American English to forestall the Trojan burrito would turn American into a frightened tongue, a shrinking little oyster tongue, as French has lately become, priested over by the Ancients of the Academie, who fret so about le weekend.* (p. 112)

Spanglish's critics view Spanglish as a dirty dialect that threatens to pollute Spanish and English. This is always the first salvo. If Spanglish has no legitimacy, it has no authenticity. We now have permission to abuse and destroy it. This criticism appeals viscerally to us because of our own distrust and suspicion of the human condition. Spanglish emerges as a debased language form—a product of backward and primitive peoples. This is why its critics believe that it has no ability to produce great literature and why they harp on social class issues. For instance, Gonzalez Echevarria (1997) says, "The sad reality is that Spanglish is primarily the language of poor Hispanics, many barely literate in either language. They incorporate English words and constructions into their daily speech because they lack the vocabulary and education in Spanish to adapt to the changing culture around them" (p. A.29). He also fears that various groups would carve out their own Spanglish, "creating a Babel of hybrid tongues" (p. A.29).

But when was language ever pure? Linguistic purity, as even Gonzalez Echevarria (1997) acknowledges, is an illusion. It is an ideological artifact. Languages are inherently promiscuous—a promiscuity that reflects us bending and twisting and recreating language to speak to new and different experiences and influences. This is why, for instance, Spanish can be so different from one place to the next. Linguistic impurity speaks to the ever evolving and changing nature of language to be inclusive rather than exclusive. As long as human beings use language, linguistic impurity will be the order of language. To attempt to keep any language pure is simply to promote the demise of that language. But more than that, language purity is really about clinging to racial purity and ideological stability. It is about the promotion of exclusion and the preservation of the status quo. Thus in linguistic impurity we find ethnic and racial impurity. We find our impulse to move beyond the separation and fragmentation that ethnic and racial purity promotes and perpetuates. We can always settle for bilingualism. But bilingualism is merely about access to different spaces. Spanglish takes us much further. It represents the mutual joining and sharing of spaces and places. This is why we *all* have to fight for Spanglish. In doing so we declare that we want more than the superficial inclusion that the status quo eventually offers those it can no longer keep marginalized. This is the only way we can truly create a space that embraces our becoming. As Morales (2002) notes, "The mixing of language that occurs in Spanglish is a metaphor for the mixture of race; it allows for races to have different voices in the same language, eliminating the need to structure language, or thinking, in terms of racial category" (p. 48).

Spanglish is what we need in an increasingly multicultural world. It shows us linguistically, communicatively, and epistemologically forging the means to find harmony in this world. This is why Spanglish is emerging and blossoming in the most heterogeneous spaces and places in the world, like New York and Los Angeles. This is also why Spanglish is emerging from the bottom social and economic classes—those persons who lack the economic means to spatially avoid other peoples by moving out to affluent hyper-suburbs and gated-communities. Exclusion is an option only for those persons who are economically privileged. But exclusion is also death. Inclusion is the order of organic systems. It represents interconnectedness and embeddedness. It also represents the end of isolation and rejection. Spanglish is about the rise of inclusion in a world where exclusion, unfortunately, is status quo. Its blatant and bold inclusion of two distinct languages speaks to an inclusion that wants nothing to do with the assimilation that so many persons who craft national policy believe is the only way to deal with an increasingly diverse U.S. society. In fact, Spanglish moves us boldly beyond the assimilation/toleration divide. We no longer have to claim, as even many prominent defenders of toleration do, that one is merely the lesser of two evils. That is, we no longer have to make believe that an increasingly diverse society requires morally awkward and imperfect frameworks to maintain peace and prosperity.

Spanglish introduces a definition of inclusion that is devoid of the reactionary tendency that characterizes both toleration and assimilation politics. What inclusion requires is evolution, or the end of separation and fragmentation. In fact, inclusion has always been the order of the world. We have always been interconnected. Buddhists, Hindus, and Jains have been teaching this reality for hundred of years. The separation we cling to is illusory, and will always be illusory. Our quest for exclusion, either racial, linguistic, ethnic, and spatial, is therefore also illusory. We will always be interconnected. The issue is one of degree. How interconnected and embedded are we willing to be? How steadfast are we going to remain to promoting and reifying the illusion of separation and fragmentation? How much of a price are we willing to pay to sustain to this illusion?

The problem with both assimilation and toleration politics is that both assume separation is the order of the world. This is why both stances are fraught with all kinds of intractable contradictions. This is also the problem that plagues bilingualism, biracialism, and biculturalism. To be global, rather than merely bicultural and multicultural, requires a different ontological footing—that footing being that we are inherently and irreversibly interconnected.

Discussion

When I look at the world, I see a vicious contest between inclusion and union (the natural striving of life) and exclusion and fragmentation (all that comes from our inability to work through our fear of the world's ambiguity). I see the rise of exclusion and fragmentation best in the rise of gated-communities and hyper-suburbs. I also see the rise of exclusion and fragmentation in the widening gap between rich and poor, both locally and globally. On the other hand, I see the rise of inclusion and union in our fight to end the world's many caste systems and to end apartheid. If, however, the gated-community and the hyper-suburb represent the most physical expression of the rise of exclusion, Spanglish arguably represents the most physical expression of inclusion. This is why, in the end, Ed Morales's (2002) *Spanglish* makes for much more compelling reading than Richard Rodriguez's (2002b) *Brown*.

Rodriguez (2002b) believes that our redemption resides in the brown peoples that miscegenation produces. Through the rise of this brown race we will ultimately end the various racisms that have long bedeviled us. Rodriguez (2002b) has no interest in interrogating the deep ideological apparatuses that promote separation, exclusion, and inequality. He is fixated with race. He also has no interest in either cosmology or ontology. Ed Morales, on the other hand, is all about cosmology and ontology. This is why he uniquely recognizes that Spanglish is more than a language. Even Illan Stavans (2000b), who is cited in nearly every media report about Spanglish as the leading authority on the subject, treats Spanglish as merely a language that deserves a semblance of acceptance. In locating Spanglish at the level of ontology—"*Living in Spanglish*"—Morales shows an ambition to disrupt the status quo. Rodriguez (2002b) has no such ambition. He wants recognition and appreciation of the browning of the U.S. Other than that, Rodriguez (2002b) has no issue with the U.S. In fact, he absolutely adores Richard Nixon.

No doubt, the U.S. is browning and this change will significantly impact U.S. society. But to reduce this browning to purely a racial phenomenon is to downplay what this browning is and what the rise of brown *really* means for the U.S. Brown is the color of creation. The rise of brown is evolutionary. It represents the end of old biases, prejudices, and suspicions. Brown is meant to disrupt the status quo, and, no doubt, Richard Rodriguez (2002b) would contend that this is happening. But Rodriguez (2002b) is under-appreciating what is happening. We are more than browning racially. We are also browning cosmologically, ontologically, epistemologically, existentially, and ideologically. Spanglish captures this browning. Spanglish is brown—very brown as a matter of fact. Rodriguez (2002b) would have us believe that brown represents an organic model of assimilation. But brown wants nothing to do with assimilation. There is no fecundity in assimilation. No possibility for revolution. No possibility for liberation. Rodriguez (2002b) makes brown palatable and fashionable. He does so by depoliticizing and defanging brown. In other words, Rodriguez

(2002b) ideologically hollows out brown. For Rodriguez (2002b), I simply represent the rise of a new race. He has no interest in my politics; that is, no concern for the forces that animate my being. Morales, however, has a fuller and better appreciation of my being. He understands and embraces the threat my brown poses to the status quo.

We will increasingly have to choose between Richard Rodriguez's brown and Ed Morales' brown. I, of course, choose the latter. I do so because inclusion is about entering the world with all of our being, and I own the fact that I am brown in my soul, in my language, in my pedagogy, and in my politics. I choose Morales' brown because I am willing to bear the burden this brown places on me.

Final Thoughts

Linguistic diversity and equality are no doubt vital to attaining and preserving human dignity and peace in the world. Unfortunately, as Lee Chong-Yeong (2003) points out in a recent issue of *The Journal of Intergroup Relations*, "Linguistic politics is increasingly becoming a destabilizing factor of world peace and justice" (p. 58). He blames "[l]inguistic hegemonism and linguistic egoism" for causing conflicts throughout the world and for promoting *linguistic incommunicability, linguistic injustice*, and *linguistic cannibalism*, all of which undermine justice and world peace. The solution to all of these problems, according to Chong-Yeong (2003), lies in the promotion of an ethnically neutral auxiliary language, such as Esperanto.

But Chong-Yeong, as with many other political scientists, makes a major theoretical error in analysis. Linguistic hegemonism and linguistic egoism are merely expressions and symptoms of larger forces that torment linguistic diversity and equality, and, by that, world peace and justice. In other words, linguistic hegemonism and linguistic egoism are artifacts of cosmological and ideological hegemonism, egoism, and chauvinism. The problem therefore has to be attacked at the cosmological and ideological level, and I would contend that doing so involves focusing beyond changing the sounds and symbols that come out of our mouths, but actually changing our relation to language and how we embody language. That is, an increasingly multicultural world demands of us a new language paradigm, and this paradigm is compellingly seen in Spanglish.

To truly achieve world peace and justice requires that we disrupt the cosmological and ideological systems which seek world domination by pushing the theoretically-flawed belief that linguistic purity, linguistic homogeneity, and linguistic stability are vital to attaining civility and progress. As long as this belief remains intact and hegemonic, linguistic diversity and equality will forever remain in peril, and thereby any possibility for world peace and justice will always elude us. As such, Spanglish gives us a new language model, as well as a new way of framing linguistic politics. Our goal, of course, should in no way be to encourage the world to adopt Spanglish. After all, left to its own organic devices and impulses, Spanglish will inherently subvert this colonization, regardless of how benevolent our intention. Instead, our goal should be to use Spanglish as a model to show other peoples throughout the world the promise of a new language model that can genuinely help attain peace and prosperity without sacrificing linguistic diversity and equality.

V

Department of Homeland Security

Writing of sacred space among the Bororo, Levi-Strauss commented on the circular arrangements of huts in their village. He claimed that this configuration was so important a fact in their social and religious life that Salesian missionaries quickly realized that the surest way to convert the Bororo was to force or entice them to abandon the form of their village in favor of one with houses arranged in parallel rows. This destruction of sacred space deprived the Indians of their bearings, subsequently causing them to lose feeling for their tradition. Levi-Strauss writes, "It was as if their social and religious systems . . . were too complex to exist without the pattern which was embodied in the plan of the village."

Richard C. Poulsen, *The Pure*
Experience of Order

The walls that ubiquitously surround us tell us to whom and where we belong, who are our friends and enemies, what is the order of the world, what is good, who is bad, what is bad, who is good. These walls shape how we experience the world, how we experience ourselves, how we experience others. So how would our humanity be different if theses walls were absent? How differently would we perceive and experience the world and each other? How different would be the world?

The separation that border walls strive to create and maintain will always be illusory. For as much as we want to continue to believe that borders are necessary for all sorts of reasons, eventually we will have to recognize that we are inextricably interconnected. We will, however, no doubt continue to believe that borders can disconnect our destinies from those on the other side. We will therefore continue to build more border walls, construct higher and higher border fences, hire more and more border guards, employ better border tracking technology, and so forth.

WASHINGTON, July 29 - Prime Minister Ariel Sharon of Israel today rebuffed pressure from President Bush to halt construction of a security fence on the West Bank . . . .Last week, the president called the fence a "problem" that could undermine efforts to build confidence between the sides; today he referred to it as a "sensitive issue" that he would continue to discuss with Mr. Sharon. . . . But more than any other issue on the table today, it was the fence - also referred to as a wall or a security barrier - that illustrated the mistrust still permeating relations between Israelis and Palestinians. The structure, concrete in some places, wire in others, already wraps around portions of the West Bank and ultimately could be hundreds of miles long. Israelis say the wall is a way of keeping suicide bombersand other attackers out . . . . On Friday, after meeting with Mr. Abbas, Mr. Bush raised the subject in remarks to reporters, and when questioned about it, said, "I think the wall is a problem," adding that he had already discussed it with Mr. Sharon. Mr. Bush said on Friday that it would be very difficult to develop confidence between Palestinians and Israelis "with a wall snaking through the West Bank." . . . "The security fence will continue to be built, with every effort to minimize the infringement on the daily life of the Palestinian population," Mr. Sharon said.

New York Times, 30 July, 2003

Arguably, what borders really do is protect us from ourselves. Borders limit our worlds by allowing us to care less, to love less, to imagine less, to give less, to empathize less. This is why walls are status quo. Walls release us from the difficult struggles that come with being fully human. Thus, as our distances and spaces increasingly collapse and contract, calls to build new security fences, to tighten our borders, and to toughen immigration laws will only heighten. But such calls only reveal a fragmentary thought system.

The wall between Israel and the West Bank will, when completed, stretch for 280 miles and possibly 403 miles. At times, it takes the form of a 26-foot-high wall, with wide buffer zones. Mostly it takes the form of a barrier 37 to 62 feet wide, which includes buffer zones, trenches and barbed wire, trace paths to register footprints, an electric fence with sensors, a two-lane patrol road and guard towers at regular intervals.

John Dugard, *The Post-Standard,*
August 10, 2003

All thoughts are inherently incomplete. That is, no thought gives a complete representation of anything. Instead, our thoughts represent various constructions of reality. For instance, two persons can look at a person fall from a building and have different experiences and interpretations of that reality. In fact, because our life experiences make us uniquely different, no two persons can ever have or share one exact frame of reference. We will always perceive and experience the world differently. But to say that our thoughts are inherently incomplete is in no way to say that our thoughts are inherently fragmentary. In fact, one has nothing to do with the other. We can have non-fragmentary thoughts. The origins of our fragmentary thought reside elsewhere. They can be found in various ideologies and cosmologies, and herein is where walls enter the equation. Walls reify and perpetuate and reinforce a fragmentary thought system by physically circumscribing how we experience and perceive the world. Case in point: the recent creation of the Department of Homeland Security.

> *Today, we are taking historic action to defend the United States and protect our citizens against the dangers of a new era. With my signature, this act of Congress will create a new Department of Homeland Security, ensuring that our efforts to defend this country are comprehensive and united.*
>
> *The new department will analyze threats, will guard our borders and airports, protect our critical infrastructure, and coordinate the response of our nation for future emergencies. The Department of Homeland Security will focus the full resources of the American government on the safety of the American people. . . . We recognize our greatest security is found in the relentless pursuit of these cold-blooded killers. Yet, because terrorists are targeting America, the front of the new war is here in America. Our life changed and changed in dramatic fashion on September the 11th, 2001. In the last 14 months, every level of our government has taken steps to be better prepared against a terrorist attack. We understand the nature of the enemy. We understand they hate us because of what we love. We're doing everything we can to enhance security at our airports and power plants and border crossings. We've deployed detection equipment to look for weapons of mass destruction. We've given law enforcement better tools to detect and disrupt terrorist cells which might be hiding in our own country. . . . With a vast nation to defend, we can neither predict nor prevent every conceivable attack. And in a free and open society, no department of government can completely guarantee our safety against ruthless killers, who move and plot in shadows. Yet our government will take every possible measure to safeguard our country and our people.*
>
> *We're fighting a new kind of war against determined enemies. And public servants long into the future will bear the responsibility to defend Americans against terror. This administration and this Congress have the duty of putting that system into place. We will fulfill that duty. With the Homeland Security Act, we're doing everything we can to protect America. We're showing the resolve of this great nation to defend our freedom, our security and our way of life. It's now my privilege to sign the Homeland Security Act of 2002. (Applause.)*
>
> Remarks by President Bush at the
> Signing of H.R. 5005, the Homeland
> Security Act of 2002

This department was created in response to the horrendous events on September 11, 2001. Its creation reflects the belief that we can somehow be kept safe from those persons who supposedly hate and envy us. Indeed, the creation of the Department, especially on heels of the events of September 11, promotes a degree of separation that gives new meaning to being Other. For instance, defending the homeland now requires that we treat all of the world's Arabs as a threat to us. We are to make believe that many Arabs simply hate us for our prosperity. Moreover, we are to believe that many Arabs, specifically those of the Muslim faith, are simply less human—which would supposedly explain why they have no moral compunction about slaughtering thousands of innocent people, and which would also apparently explain why they worship a prophet that promotes terror and misery. Such are the sins that the Department of Homeland Security now demands that millions of innocent human beings bear. It puts those of us who are supposedly of the homeland at war with the world, especially with hundreds of millions of Arabs and Muslims.

A serious war against terrorism requires both an offense and a defense. Offense means using force, in a variety of forms, to detain or destroy terrorists wherever they live, recruit, train, and plot—but before they get near their intended victims. When offense fails, defense has to kick in. Defense means homeland security, and homeland security boils down to the three G's: guards, guns, and gates.

Clifford D. May, *President,*
Foundation for the Defense
of Democracies

We now have to secure our borders, limit immigration, create new legislation that materializes the police state, and increase military funding, so as to wage war against all those who wish to hurt us. The tremendous public support for the creation of the Department of Homeland Security is significant. It speaks to the fact that many people actually believe that our homeland is being threatened by a growing race of people who supposedly lack our sense of civility and decency. After all, "what we [alone] love" is democracy and freedom. We therefore believe that we have a national interest in imposing our moral codes and institutions upon others, especially those of the Arab world. Thus the rise of the Department of Homeland Security correlates with the rise of a new U.S. imperialism. Although the White House says again and again that the U.S. has no hostility against the Arab peoples, those peoples know better. When the White House speaks about wanting to bring democracy to the Middle East, most Arabs understand that what President Bush really wants to do is to impose U.S. institutions in that region of the world. The White House's implicit message is that these people are simply incapable of developing and sustaining their own democratic institutions, along with the values, beliefs, and norms that come with democracy. In other words, the implicit message is that the people in the Middle East are incapable of developing their own civilized and decent society. We apparently have the means to do so, which is to say that we *do* have a civilized and decent society, and, apparently, the Middle East has none. As a result, we are morally—even spiritually—justified in using war and the threat of war to impose our institutions in that region. (Best-selling author Ann Coulter even said after September 11 that the U.S. should "invade their countries, kill their leaders, and convert them to Christianity"). We have seen this kind of rationalization throughout history, as in the case of expansionism in Hitler's Germany. No doubt the rest of the world has a right to be afraid of the U.S.

Today, we take an essential step in defeating terrorism, while protecting the constitutional rights of all Americans. With my signature, this law will give intelligence and law enforcement officials important new tools to fight a present danger. . . .

The changes, effective today, will help counter a threat like no other our nation has ever faced. We've seen the enemy, and the murder of thousands of innocent, unsuspecting people. They recognize no barrier of morality. They have no conscience. The terrorists cannot be reasoned with. . . .

But one thing is for certain: These terrorists must be pursued, they must be defeated, and they must be brought to justice. (Applause.) And that is the purpose of this legislation. Since the 11th of September, the men and women of our intelligence and law enforcement agencies have been relentless in their response to new and sudden challenges.

We have seen the horrors terrorists can inflict. We may never know what horrors our country was spared by the diligent and determined work of our police forces, the FBI, ATF agents, federal marshals, Custom officers, Secret Service, intelligence professionals and local law enforcement officials, under the most trying conditions. They are serving this country with excellence, and often with bravery.

They deserve our full support and every means of help that we can provide. We're dealing with terrorists who operate by highly sophisticated methods and technologies, some of which were not even available when our existing laws were written. The bill before me takes account of the new realities and dangers posed by modern terrorists. It will help law enforcement to identify, to dismantle, to disrupt, and to punish terrorists before they strike. . . .

This legislation is essential not only to pursuing and punishing terrorists, but also preventing more atrocities in the hands of the evil ones. This government will enforce this law with all the urgency of a nation at war. The elected branches of our government, and both political parties, are united in our resolve to fight and stop and punish those who would do harm to the American people.

It is now my honor to sign into law the USA Patriot Act of 2001. (Applause.)

> Remarks by President Bush at Signing of the
> Patriot Act, Anti-Terrorism Legislation

The Department of Homeland Security makes believe that we are justified in being afraid of the world. The world's barbarians are supposedly at our gates—threatening to destroy and undermine the institutions that make for our "unsurpassed greatness." Naturally, sacrifices are required on our part. We have to be willing to give up various rights and privileges to allow our government to win this war and, thereby, allow us to save the homeland from the barbarians.

Thus the legislation that accompanies the creation of the Department of Homeland Security is aptly titled the Patriot Act. Now we can easily label and identity those persons who are aiding and abetting the enemy by their refusal to surrender various rights and privileges that are necessary to protect the homeland. It is no longer enough to be a citizen of the homeland. Now we have to be patriots, and zealous ones at that. We have to be ready to fight and do all that is necessary to defend the homeland, even if that means contributing to the creation of a police state.

This is how our thought system works. Notice the perpetuation of separation. Notice the promotion of fragmentation. Notice also the distortions and the illusions. In the end, the Department of Homeland Security does nothing to protect us. It only succeeds in making the U.S. the world's largest gated community. But why do various people, who Ann Coulter casually refers to as third world savages, wish to inflict misery and suffering upon us? Why is the rest of the world increasingly against us? In fact, what about our own morality is so obviously superior? What about the terrorism we have perpetrated throughout the world for our own purely selfish self-interest? What about our support for the world's most hideous regimes? What about the slavery that was for so long legal in the homeland? What also about the apartheid system that was, until lately, also legal in the homeland? The Department of Homeland Security releases us from asking these kinds of questions. We are subtly discouraged from asking why the rest of the world increasingly hates us. Instead, the Department of Homeland Security encourages us to believe that we are simply morally superior, and, as such, can do as we please, especially when it comes to our own security and our own self-interest. As such, President Bush's imperialism continues to enjoy large public support. We actually believe that war will give us our security. We are told again and again that war is the only language that our opponents understand, which of course reinforces the view that we are dealing with people who are morally inferior to us. So we are now set on a path of war and more war. As we wage war in Iraq and Afghanistan, we are also at the same time threatening to wage war in Iran and Syria. The creation of the Department of Homeland Security has set off a new arms race. To stop U.S. aggression, now more and more nations—who of course never needed any encouragement to begin with—are rushing to acquire nuclear weapons, even though such acquisition comes at the cost of further misery for millions of people. Obviously, nothing good can come from this arms escalation.

We are already on the brink of a war that will end all wars. We simply cannot war our way to peace and security. The thought system behind the Department of Homeland Security puts us down a perilous path. What, however, is the legitimacy of any thought system that would do this to us? President Bush speaks again and again about staying the course. But—ultimately—at what cost?

Our thoughts will always be inherently incomplete. But our thoughts can also become more complete and thereby less fragmentary. In fact, only by becoming more complete can we realize our redemption. In this way, the challenge of completion is fundamental to being human, or at least to becoming more human. It is the primary burden we bear. But to speak about the notion of incomplete thought is also a bit misleading. We are really speaking of an entire thought system. We are speaking about a consciousness, a way of being and engaging and experiencing and embodying the world. To speak of a thought system is to make believe that our thoughts originate in mental and cognitive processes. But to do so is to perpetuate a fragmentary consciousness by—again—making believe that the way we understand the world is purely a mental and cognitive process, a process separate from other dimensions that make us human. Though we have sought to isolate and privilege our mental and cognitive processes, no thought system, no knowledge system, no consciousness, is ever devoid of emotional, existential, relational, sensual, historical, and spiritual processes. Even to speak of these processes separately is an illusion.

Yet we pay a tremendous price for maintaining the illusion that our thought systems are mental and cognitive in nature. This is an illusion of convenience. To view our thoughts as mental artifacts limits our understanding of the world, retards how we engage the world, and, ultimately, distorts our knowledge of the world. What emerges is the belief the world lends itself to easy and simple equations—ones that demand nothing much from us. As such, neither our epistemology nor our methodology comes to demand anything from us. We remain of the belief that the secrets of the world can be discovered in our robust and objective methods. Knowledge generation emerges as an abstract and objective process that occurs outside of us. We merely need to possess the necessary cognitive capacity to process data. Intelligence therefore comes to be defined as a mental and cognitive artifact, to be measured as a cognitive quotient. Even our pedagogical practices focus on enhancing our cognitive capacity and making us superior cognitive automatons.

> *No part of the aim of normal science is to call forth new sorts of phenomena; indeed those that will not fit the box are often not seen at all. Nor do scientists normally aim to invent new theories, and they are often intolerant of those invented by others. Instead, normal-scientific research is directed to the articulation of those phenomena and theories that the paradigm already supplies.*
>
> Thomas Kuhn, *The Nature Of Scientific Revolutions*

No doubt, we have a lot invested in this thought system. Our truths, our understanding of the world, our sciences, our social, educational, and political systems, are all riding on this thought system. If this thought system collapses, the status quo collapses. We therefore have a natural hostility to new and different thought systems; such systems will always pose a threat to the status quo. This is the debt we owe Thomas Kuhn. He eloquently explains to us how science ideologically subverts the evolution of new knowledge. One key way is by emphasizing recovery rather than discovery. Recovery requires no interrogation of the world. We merely employ norms, assumptions, beliefs, truths, and so forth that already exist. After all, we already know what we are going to find.

> *Normal science, the activity in which most scientists inevitably spend almost all their time, is predicted on the assumption that the scientific community knows what the world is like. Much of the success of the enterprise derives from the community's willingness to defend that assumption, if necessary at considerable cost. Normal science, for example, often suppresses fundamental novelties because they are necessarily subversive of its basic commitments. . . .*
>
> *The group's members, as individuals and by virtue of their shared training and experience, must be seen as the sole possessors of the rules of the game or of some equivalent basis for unequivocal judgments. To doubt that they shared some such basis for evaluations would be to admit the existence of incompatible standards of scientific achievement. That admission would inevitably raise the question of whether truth in the sciences can be one.*
>
> Thomas Kuhn, *The Nature Of*
> *Scientific Revolutions*

To change our truths and understanding of the world therefore requires that we change our thought system. In fact, changing our thought system is the only way to really interrupt the status quo. But the status quo will seek to suppress all threats to its integrity. It gains nothing from change. This is why, as Kuhn explains, our sciences never encourage discovery. To accept the possibility of new truths, new understandings, new realities, and new possibilities is to accept the fact that our present truths, understandings, and so forth are inherently unstable and incomplete; even possibly wrong. We will be forced to be more sensitive and open to other peoples' truths and understandings. Our imperialist ambition would be undercut. We would inevitably become more humble and vulnerable, and thereby less divorced from the complexity and ambiguity of our own humanity and that of the world. In this way, our present thought system spares us from openly engaging the world's ambiguity, complexity, and mystery. It allows us to make believe that we can be gods; and gods, no doubt, we have sought to be.

David Bohm believes that most physicists who work with—and even teach—quantum physics really have no understanding of the ideological and cosmological implications that come with quantum theory. That is, most are yet to understand that quantum theory really represents a completely new thought system. Even Noble Laureate Steven Weinberg claims that quantum theory represents no evolution of a new paradigm. For Weinberg and many other prominent physicists, quantum theory is merely another way of doing physics. Evidently, the status quo's thought system is being imposed on quantum theory. We are viewing quantum theory from the standpoint that we are emotionally and existentially ready and willing to view quantum theory. So instead of quantum theory appearing to us as a new worldview, it emerges as merely another way of doing physics. Our own fragmentary thought system succeeds in emasculating and co-opting quantum theory. It strips quantum theory of all its cosmological, ideological, social, and political gravitas.

Of course to speak about our own thought system is really to speak about us. Until we are emotionally, existentially, and even spiritually ready to look at the world differently, the world will always appear to us how we want and need it to appear to us. Our theories and methods are merely artifacts of being. It is at the level of being that knowledge begins and remains. If we wish to change our knowledge of the world, or to develop a new knowledge of the world, we have to be willing to change our ways of being and engaging the world. But we want to have nothing to do with being. It is too complex. This is why Kuhn had such a tough time explaining how paradigm shifts occur. In one way, Kuhn was describing how science works and paradigm shifts occur, but in another way he was really describing *us* and the hegemony of our own thought system.

Paradigm change occurs haphazardly because we fight and resist the evolution of new ways of being so as to spare us from dealing with the world's complexity and ambiguity. We are ontologically and epistemologically set to experience the world in ways that stress recovery rather than discovery. It takes an extraordinary amount of courage to violate this process. Other times, as Kuhn explains, paradigm shifts occur gradually. Unanticipated discoveries simply push us to abandon dominant frameworks. Other times, long held explanations slowly succumb to the world's complexity and ambiguity. None of these processes we readily embrace. We will therefore always torment, as Einstein told us we would, those persons who challenge us to look differently at the world.

The Marriage Between Space and Knowledge

So how exactly does space function to preserve our thought systems? How does space function in our thought system to undermine the evolution of new thought systems and new types of being? How could we construct space to make for more complete thought systems? I often try to imagine the world without walls, borders, and fences. I wonder what would be absent in this world. What discursive practices would be nonexistent? What discursive practices would I have that I lack now? How would my discursive world be different? It is, no doubt, hard to imagine this world. It seems impossible, even existentially impossible. It seems that I am trying to do something that is simply unnatural. But I believe this supposed unnaturalness merely reflects the deep fragmentation that permeates my being.

In reality, I am in no way merely trying to imagine a physical world. What I am really trying to do is to embody a different thought system, one that is dramatically less fragmentary than my own. This is why the task is so daunting. My present thought system is inherently hostile to one that is so different and contradictory to it. I am supposed to have no imagination of this wall-less, borderless, and fenceless world. It should appear unnatural to me. So what do I do? What do we do? It would be nice to have the ability to simply drop one thought system and pick up another. But thought systems reside at the core of our being. We therefore have to evolve towards a more expansive thought system. We have to gradually acquire the emotional, mental, spiritual, existential, and sensual disposition that constitutes such thought systems. To embody more expansive thought systems requires us to be much more resilient so that we can better grapple with the ambiguity and complexity that come with such thought systems. So, for now, I am unable to visualize a world without walls, borders, and fences. It will continue to appear unnatural to me. But my inability to imagine this world—in no way—means that this world is impossible. It is possible, and thus dialogue enters the redemption equation.

David Bohm believes that dialogue is our path towards a more complete thought system. Bohm is, of course, defining dialogue differently than we commonly define dialogue. Instead of a way of speaking and conversing, dialogue is a way of being in the world that is committed to the promotion of new realties and possibilities. That is, dialogue is about communication as humanity building, communication as knowledge building, and communication as world making. Bohm contends that, because the world is neither finite nor constant, there is no set knowledge out there for us to discover, like the way a miner mines for gold; nor is the world separate and apart from us. There is therefore no *real* usefulness in any methodology or epistemology that rests on any of these assumptions.

What the world *is* is determined by what we are, and in turn what we are is determined by what we are ready and willing to be. Thus, to assume or to believe that the world is finite and constant is to believe that we are also finite and constant. For instance, to believe that our destinies are set by what souls we inherit, or what biology (e.g., gender and race) we inherit, or what essences we inherit is to also believe, as history shows, that the world is finite and constant— either through the workings of a God, nature, or some other force. To speak of a finite world is to really speak about a world with a finite set of possibilities and realities. Thus throughout history we have declared—with the authority of a God no doubt—at different periods, the order of world, and used this *knowledge* to organize our societies in finite ways.

In a finite world, communication emerges simply as a process that facilitates the flow of messages within societies between persons whose fates are also finite. Moreover, within a finite world, space too is finite. We therefore strive to possess space, to horde space, to protect and demarcate our space with walls, fences, and borders. If space is finite, and thereby precious, then war is no doubt a viable option in laying claim to space. In fact, a finite world promotes war and aggression by encouraging us to fight over its finite truths and resources. We also must war over which truths will organize our societies, and which truths will determine who gets what space and how much space.

The Palestinian/Israeli conflict bears all of this out well. Both sides contend that God has given them the land that they now war over. As such, both sides claim to have a divine right to the land and a divine right to defend the land at any cost. The conflict therefore appears intractable and unsolvable. After all, how could either side surrender what they believe God has divinely given to them? As a result, the only recourse for either side is to war over the land. What other option is there? In a finite world, God is also finite, and so are knowledge and truth. There is supposedly no possibility for a completely new and different reality—one that is outside of what our finite world ordains. We simply have to accept what is the nature of the world and find our peace within it. A finite world ontologically discourages us from believing in radically new possibilities and realities. Thus many Israelis and Palestinians believe war is only one way out of this conflict. Others on both sides believe that peace will depend on both sides being ready to live with imperfect solutions.

A finite world undermines imagination, innovation, and knowledge creation. Knowledge creation is limited to discovery—discovering what already resides in the world—and authenticating discoveries. This is why, as Kuhn compellingly explains, science has no interest in the pursuit of new knowledge. In a finite world, how could we possibly approach knowledge differently? How could we possibly have different definitions of knowledge? How could we have different methodologies and epistemologies? More importantly, how can we acknowledge and even reward other definitions of knowledge?

We will come to a world without walls, fences, and borders, only when we come to a worldview that assumes an infinite world—one that allows for an infinite set of possibilities and realities. Until then, our thought system will legitimize only that knowledge that re-inscribes a finite world. Those persons who embody other thought systems, and thereby forward different kinds of knowledge of the world, will simply have to continue to fight to remain sane. Such is the order of the world as dictated by our present thought system.

The Dawning of a New Knowledge

All paradigms eventually change. We are forced to look at the world differently for one reason or another. This is what quantum theory is forcing us to do now, regardless of the protestations of many proponents of the status quo. The revolution is on. We are within the throes of a new paradigm. New observations are undermining long held beliefs. David Bohm's life work was about describing the full implication of this emergent paradigm that is upon us. How is this paradigm re-describing our world? What realities and possibilities come with this emergent world? How do we produce knowledge in this new paradigm? How do we define knowledge? How do we distinguish false knowledge from true knowledge? Dialogue is at the heart of all of these questions. We are increasingly less beholden to the view that the world is finite and constant. Mechanical metaphors no longer work in describing the world for more and more of us. Instead, we are increasingly coming around to the view that the world is infinite in nature.

There are many factors contributing to the evolution to this new thought system. One such factor is that we are simply becoming less afraid of what it means to be human and thus more open to new ways of perceiving and experiencing the world. Another factor is simply our increased accessibility to other peoples with different thought systems. Another factor we can probably describe as the existential or spiritual factor, or what Robert Torrance refers to as our spiritual questing—our inherent evolutionary striving to transcend the present. Finally, the world is no longer legitimizing commonly held explanations of the world. These explanations are no longer proving adequate in accounting for how the world works. Even our best efforts to keep them in tact can do nothing to stop their gradual implosion. It seems that ever so often the world insists on reminding us that it will always reject those explanations that attempt to defy its infinite potentiality. So again and again we have to reckon with this potentiality, which means being baffled by anomalies and discoveries that come out of nowhere and simply make no sense to us.

Still, what keeps our fragmentary thought system status quo is that it undermines and limits new explanations of our humanity. Paradigms change because, ultimately, the explanations we use to make sense of ourselves no longer suffice. We are forced to recognize that there is more to our humanity, more we are capable of understanding and doing and, as a result, more the world is capable of. That we now stand on the threshold of a paradigm that explicitly posits notions of an infinite world is really about us now coming to a point in history where we are finally ready and willing to transcend all the markers that we have long used to limit our humanity. In this way, the world's infiniteness is really about our infiniteness. We are more and more coming to the recognition that our own potentiality is infinite. We are therefore more capable of constructing worlds outside the purview of worlds where our fates are predetermined.

Never before have we so openly and aggressively defied the status quo, on the threshold of a knowledge system that breaks completely with dominant knowledge systems that have always managed to maintain a level of continuity in the face of many disruptions. Naturally, the reaction of the status quo is to push fear. We are to be afraid of the coming anarchy that will come when the barbarians take over the castle. Academe, as always, remains determined to protect the status quo by insisting on being the referees of what constitutes legitimate knowledge and anointing those who are to be the guardians of this knowledge. Those persons found cohorting with the barbarians and pushing illicit thoughts come to be persona non grata in academe. But such drastic action can do nothing to stop the revolution that is upon us. The reason being that this paradigm shift is occurring on the streets, in our homes, among our friends, in our day-to-day lives, with our lovers, in hallways, in airports, on sidewalks, and nearly everywhere else where worlds are colliding. It can also be seen between the Israeli guy and his Palestinian girlfriend, the Japanese woman and her Indian boyfriend, and the Puerto Rican woman and her Chinese lover. This is an emergent and organic paradigm shift. Our collapsing spaces and distances are forcing us, in one way or the other, to confront and deal with each other. We are beginning to demystify each other, and beginning to appreciate other ways of understanding and experiencing the world. Ultimately, what we are really doing is demystifying what it means to be human; that is, becoming less afraid of our own humanity. In beginning to put down our fears of people who are supposed to be so strange and alien to us, we are becoming more and more wary of the thought system that wants us to believe that there is no common humanity between these peoples and us.

But the status quo caught a break on September 11th. The events of this day supposedly show that our humanities are indeed separate and different. This is why we need to retain the status quo—to protect ourselves from the savages who hate and envy us. In this way the events of September 11th are historically and paradigmatically significant. These events are now used to re-engender a deep fear of all humanity so as to keep us bound to the status quo. We must believe that some realities are simply inescapable, including war and the institutions that come with waging war. We must also believe that the world is in no way laden with infinite possibilities and realities, and those persons who push this idea are simply hacks and fools. We are reminded again and again that those persons who crashed those planes into those buildings were real. But even in the face of U.S. imperialism, the revolution is still on, as seen in the unison of reaction throughout the world against U.S. waging war in Iraq. Never before have so many of the world's different peoples spoken in such unison. Never before have so many peoples been seen to be of one space and place. We will not be ruled by one truth, one God, one religion, one worldview, one science.

VI

On Fragmentation & Union

We are increasingly heeding the reality that spaces and places that promote fragmentation and division undermine innovation by limiting human interaction and communication. As such, many new buildings are devoid of walls and cubicles. The focus now is on a design ecology that fosters human interaction and communication. This new ecology also incorporates new kinds of furniture. Increasingly, our goal in organizing human beings is no longer to limit interaction and communication so as to maintain order and control.

But of course paradigms are hard to change. We still believe that the primary purpose of organizing is to maintain order and control, and we still seek to do so by controlling and limiting interaction and communication. We also still have a deep distrust and suspicion of our humanity. Our organizing goal is to limit our supposed proclivity for chaos and destruction. We therefore have long been trying to get our organizing to exercise superior kinds of order and control. We also still commonly assume that organizing is a means to an end. We organize so as to perform functions that require collective effort and will. Organizing supposedly has no moral, existential, or spiritual origin. Its origins are purely in necessity—born out of our evolutionary need for coordination and collective action. Our spaces and designs therefore stress utility and functionality.

But new understandings of the world are releasing us of many of the assumptions that shape our common understanding of organizing. We are more and more recognizing that this is an inherently organizing world, one that is always organizing. Organizing brings harmony to the world. It is an inherently relational phenomenon, which is to say that organizing constitutes the world relationally. It is within relationships that life resides and finds meaning and expression. So the condition of the world can always be measured by the quantity and quality of relationships that are found in the world. This reality is aptly seen in natural systems. We measure the condition of a forest, for example, by identifying whether new relationships are increasing or declining. If new relationships are emerging, this means that life forms in the system are prospering, and also that new life forms are emerging in the system. It also means that the system is attaining complexity and diversity and, in so doing, prospering. Conversely, when the condition of a system is declining, both tend to disappear. Organizing therefore brings complexity and diversity to the world. It gives life expression.

But again, paradigms are hard to change. We still assume no moral or spiritual relation between the world and us. We are supposedly unbound from the natural rhythms and movements that strive to foster life's evolution and expansion. We therefore assume that organizing has no inherent moral or spiritual calculus or striving, and that our goal to make organizing less and less complex and more and more homogenous comes with no consequences and implications. In fact, we still assume that the world has nothing to teach us about organizing. But we err in assuming that increasing interaction improves organizing. We also err in using interaction and communication interchangeably. Only communication is constitutive. Good communication calls forth a humanity that can exercise deep levels of compassion, openness, and hope. This humanity can only be forged by a willingness to risk life. Increasing interaction demands no risking of life. It makes no demands on our humanity and, as a result, poses no threat to the status quo. New spaces and designs that aim simply to increase interaction therefore pose no threat to us. Such designs are premised on the view that the origins of communication are in necessity and utility. Supposedly, we can improve communication by merely changing our spaces and designs. We also err in assuming that good organizing requires clarity of thought and expression, and that we can improve organizing by merely increasing human interaction. In short, our living, working, socializing, and learning spaces are changing only out of necessity. We are merely making architectural alterations and only for reasons of promoting innovation. We are yet to fully understand that organizing is the means by which life finds both expression and meaning. To look at communication as the constitutive process of being human politicizes the organization of our spaces. The organization of our spaces and places affects the condition of our humanity and, conversely, the condition of our humanity influences the organization of our spaces and places. In this way, our spaces and designs bare our souls to the world. We need spaces and designs that allow us to move in accord with the natural rhythms of the world, that promote diversity and complexity, that foster hope, openness, and compassion, that make us less afraid of the world and each other, that heal and nourish us, and that lessen the threat of our differences by encouraging us to pay attention to our common humanness and humanity. These spaces and designs will only materialize in organizing models that move us beyond our obsession with hierarchically imposing order and control upon other human beings.

VII

Space & Ecology

There is increasing discussion about the population explosion that the planet is witnessing and the perilous threats that it poses to our survival as a species. Overpopulation is seen by many scholars and policy analysts as the most serious threat that the planet faces. There are urgent calls for governments to intervene and stop this explosion. We are told again and again about the correlation between the rise of our population levels and the deterioration of the planet's biodiversity. Indeed, news reports are often laden with disturbing images of various Third World peoples starving of malnutrition, clearing-cutting forests, and attending to numerous hungry and badly-deformed children.

The key to understanding overpopulation is not population density but the numbers of people in an area relative to its resources and the capacity of the environment to sustain human activities; that is, to the area's carrying capacity. When is an area overpopulated? When its population can't be maintained without rapidly depleting nonrenewable resources (or converting renewable resources into nonrenewable ones) and without degrading the capacity of the environment to support the population. In short, if the long-term carrying capacity of an area is clearly being degraded by its current human occupants, that area is overpopulated.

By this standard, the entire planet and virtually every nation is already vastly overpopulated. Africa is overpopulated now because, among other indications, its soils and forests are rapidly being depleted—and that implies that its carrying capacity for human beings will be lower in the future than it is now. The United States is overpopulated because it is depleting its soil and water resources and contributing mightily to the destruction of global environmental systems. Europe, Japan, the Soviet Union, and other rich nations are overpopulated because of their massive contributions to the carbon dioxide buildup in the atmosphere, among many other reasons.

Almost all the rich nations are overpopulated because they are rapidly drawing down stocks of resources around the world. They don't live solely on the land in their own nations. Like the profligate son of our earlier analogy, they are spending their capital with no thought for the future.

Paul and Anne Ehrlich,
The Population Explosion

Overpopulation does threaten the planet's biodiversity and its prosperity. The planet only has so much habitable and livable space. But what needs to concern us is how the problem—the planet's ecological peril—is being configured and why is it being configured the way it is being configured. In short, we need to focus on the deep ideological practices that are shaping our understanding of the planet's peril; specifically, with how a hierarchical—and by that a fragmented—consciousness remains embedded within discourses about this peril. Such discourses relegitimize hierarchy by reinforcing our deep distrust and suspicion of the human condition. We assume, as always, that without hierarchy we will supposedly descend—in this case through overpopulation—towards chaos and destruction. We therefore believe that we need to hierarchically and coercively impose practices on ourselves and others to stop our supposed malevolent proclivity to overpopulate. In this way, we continue to believe that hierarchy is integral to our prosperity and that of the planet.

Our procreative habits are threatening nature; fortunately, we can do something about it. The greatest conservation measure that human beings can take is to halt the growth of our population. It is the only way we can sustain ourselves and the planet's ecological health.

Jeffrey K. McKee,
Ohio State University

Our configuration of the planet's peril in terms of overpopulation therefore poses no threat to the status quo. It allows us to sustain our deepest beliefs and suspicions of the human condition: such as the belief that we possess a proclivity for chaos and destruction, and thus hierarchy is natural and even vital for our prosperity. It also requires no risking of life, no forging on our part of new and different ways of being in the world. It merely requires minor alterations, such as the use of more renewable energy sources, more recycling, more conservation of natural resources, more replanting of trees, more legislation, and so forth. Such alterations pose no threat to the dominant social, political, spatial, and ideological order. As such, this order escapes interrogation and responsibility for the condition of the planet. In other words, this dominant configuration poses no threat to us. It allows us to continue to believe that we are separate from the world, that our social, political, and intellectual is inherently good and superior to others, and that the burden for the planet's peril can be put on others. There is no reason or incentive for us to forge a new psychology and sociology.

We show a shallow understanding of the human condition when we configure the planet's problems in terms of overpopulation. We assume no faith in our potential to make for a new and better world. In fact, we assume that no such potential exists. We look outside of the human condition for ways to create and sustain morality and civility. We assume that our redemption resides in the institutions and structures that we create and hierarchically impose upon others, ourselves, and even upon the planet. Through our institutions we will bring order upon the world and thereby make for our progress and prosperity.

So in the case of the world's exploding population and the ending of the planet's biodiversity, we believe that the solution resides either in the institutions and structures of governments or in capitalist/market systems. But putting our redemption in the hands of such structures and institutions releases us of any responsibility for our own redemption. We relegitimize the belief that we have no inherent potential or capacity for redemption. That is, our common understanding of what constitutes the good society undermines the evolution of our humanity by putting no onus on us to look within ourselves and engage in the necessary hard work that comes with the expansion of our humanity, such as building the relations and designing the spaces that promote trust, empathy, compassion, openness, forgiveness, and so forth. It promotes our separation from each other and the world by discouraging us from directly engaging each other and the world. The result is us being afraid of our own humanity and lacking any faith in our ability to change the world.

We believe that change must come institutionally—through our institutions, we will change the world. Of course, nowhere is this mentality more evident than in the rise of global capitalism and the accompanying rise of the grand international institutions and structures that will supposedly make for the world's progress and prosperity though global capitalism. These institutions aim to develop and employ practices that overwhelm and conquer local institutions in order to make for the homogeneity that is vital to the rise of global capitalism. In fact, these institutions are increasingly bestowing upon corporations legal rights and privileges that exceed those legally given to human beings. The result being that these institutions and corporations are collapsing and homogenizing space though the imposition of global capitalism.

Institutions evolve out of us trying to sustain the status quo so as to avoid dealing with the world's infinite ambiguity. We strive to block change, new vistas of being, and the natural quantum rhythms of life. But this ambition comes at a perilous cost. In blocking evolution, institutions undermine life's diversity, beauty, and prosperity and, in so doing, undermine life's complexity and resiliency. We lose the mental, emotional, and spiritual resiliency to forge deep and complex relations—relations that are inherently nonhierarchical. This is why so much dysfunctionality and deviancy attend to institutional life. Ultimately, institutions do nothing good for us.

It is, however, our fixation with institutions, and the worldview that promotes this fixation and hegemony, that is most responsible for the planet's peril. Institutions block the expansion of our humanity, which is necessary for us to develop the ways of being that make for the practices and behaviors that complement, rather than destroy, the planet's biodiversity. It is only through this expansion that we recognize our embeddedness in the world. Thus, to save the planet's biodiversity requires us to come to a new understanding of diversity— one that recognizes that life only flourishes when diversity flourishes. Our institutional fixation undercuts an emergent understanding of diversity by tying homogeneity to unity and stability. We assume a deep suspicion of diversity. We believe that diversity needs to be controlled and managed and tolerated so as to avoid disunity and instability. Further, institutions undercut the evolution of diversity by undermining the mental, emotional, and spiritual resiliency that promotes diversity. Diversity requires all the practices—empathy, compassion, trust, flexibility, openness, and so forth—that institutions undercut by promoting structures rather than relationships. Diversity resides between human beings, rather than being something that we possess. This relation is characterized by empathy, compassion, openness, and trust. It is a relation that catalyzes the evolution of new and different ways of being. In sum, diversity reflects relations that allow for the communion of differences.

To cast the planet's problems in terms of overpopulation therefore masks the complexity of the problems that the planet faces and diminishes the complexity of the solution. Even reducing the planet's population by half does nothing to stop the peril the planet faces. Our belief that the world is in conflict with us puts us at odds with the planet's biodiversity. No amount of recycling, replanting, and conservation will stop the threat that this belief poses to the planet's biodiversity. Neither does our masking of the complexity of the problem delay our day of reckoning. To believe that we are in conflict with the world assumes that our survival and prosperity require that we win this conflict. The result is a hostile stance towards the world.

But we remain bent on maintaining the status quo. We are promoting recycling, replanting, and other conservation initiatives to the hilt. We are encouraging investments in renewable energy resources, working to limit the emission of dangerous pollutants, and trying to encourage more earth-friendly initiatives. We are also enacting legislation to protect wetlands, old forests, rivers, and so forth. We are even pressing our governments to fund family planning programs that limit the overpopulation that supposedly poses such a perilous threat to the planet. We no doubt recognize that we need to make lifestyle changes. Yet such changes hardly suffice to stop our destruction of the planet's biodiversity. Again, the reason being that such changes pose no threat to the status quo. Thus we are still making no connection between the condition of our humanity and the condition of the world. We still assume that no such connection exists. Saving the planet simply requires the implementation of reasonable initiatives. In fact, the green movement is the status quo. It neither assumes nor articulates a new worldview. It merely wants a greener world.

So the notion of overpopulation allows us to avoid doing the hard work that comes with looking at the world differently. We can simply blame the weak and vulnerable for the planet's problems. But now this ploy is unraveling. In reality, the planet's biodiversity has long been in peril. We have long been at war with the world—resulting in our constant undermining of the planet's biodiversity. The disintegration of the planet's biodiversity is only a symptom of the problem. The human condition has long been in peril. Our war upon the world exacts a perilous toll on us. The deterioration of the planet reflects the deterioration of our own humanity. We, of course, mask the latter's destruction when we construct discourses about the planet in terms of population issues. We make believe that there is no moral, existential, or spiritual relation between our condition and that of the condition of the planet. We cast the situation in a discourse of survival, of the primal, and of the practical—recycling, replanting, conservation, and so forth is simply good business. To save the planet is to make for our survival. We assume that the unsurpassed levels of human misery and human meltdown that we are increasingly bearing witness to have no relation to the condition of the planet, or with the racism, sexism, heterosexism, classism, neo-colonialism, and other such evils that still permeate the world. These are supposedly human problems, requiring solutions that are different and apart from what the planet now requires. Such is the narrowness that shapes our discourse about the planet.

Racism finds origins and legitimacy in civilizations that need excess labor so as to plunder the planet's natural resources for selfish gain. In the western world, for example, slavery made for the expansion of practices—such as mono-cropping—that eroded a lot of the planet's biodiversity. Fascism also sought to end the planet's biodiversity—specifically the diversity found in us. Indeed, racism, sexism, colonialism, and so forth all seek to end the planet's diversity. All such evils find origin in a worldview that assumes that the world is in conflict with us and that we have a proclivity for chaos and destruction. Yet we believe that this same worldview can lead us to redemption, that is, a better relation to the planet. In fact, in reducing racism, sexism, and so forth to *just* human problems, we limit the enormity of these evils. The result is that we look in the wrong places for the origins and solutions to these problems. We will only save the planet when we end the beliefs and practices that make for these evils. As such, to assume that population explosion is the definitive problem facing the planet is to also help downplay the destructive impact of racism, sexism, and other such evils.

We need to end the false separation between the environment and human issues. This separation ill serves us. We need a new discourse. But integral to the evolution of such a discourse is the evolution of a worldview that assumes no separation between us and the world—a worldview that, obviously, poses the most serious threat to the status quo; that is, to us. Only such a worldview will make for a psychology that promotes union and communion rather than separation and fragmentation and, as a result, end the alienation that causes so much human misery. In other words, resolving our overpopulation and biodiversity peril involves the evolution of a conception of space that undermines separation and fragmentation by revealing an interconnected and embedded world. The geography of other nations will no longer be separate from our geography. We will no longer assume that Mexico's biodiversity problem is Mexico's problem, or, as in the case of the Sierra Club, make believe that closing our borders will help solve the biodiversity problem in the U.S. After all, the notion that borders and border guards make us different and separate our faiths has also been illusory. Yet we continue to believe and perpetuate this illusion because we need the separation and fragmentation that come with borders and passports. In limiting our worlds, this illusion allows us to demand less of ourselves. If indeed Mexico's biodiversity problem is just as much our problem, then we will of course have to do something completely different. But what are the alternatives? Regardless of how we choose to divide and fragment the world's geography, we will always be of one space and, thereby, always of one destiny. Thus, besides making for the biodiversity and overpopulation problem that now threatens us, our fragmented consciousness is undermining our ability to perceive the problem fully and, thereby, also undermining our ability to act in ways that are urgently necessary to solve this problem.

So we strive to preserve the status quo. The disruption that a new world-view threatens is existentially threatening. We are instinctively inclined to want order rather than chaos, stability rather than instability, convergence rather than divergence, simplicity rather than complexity, homogeneity rather than diversity, and so forth. In this way, the status quo always enjoys a privileged position. Our evolution requires the constant exercising of mental, emotional, and spiritual resiliency. Such work requires much effort. But what is the cost of preserving the status quo? In this case, we making believe that population explosion is primarily responsible for the planet's peril. What is the purchase of this belief, this distortion?

We preserve the status quo at the most perilous of costs. A new worldview that ends our separation from the world and the planet is by no means completely foreign to us. In reality, the origins and yearnings of this worldview already reside within us. We have always been embedded in the world and the world has always been embedded within us. We and the world are one and, regardless of our own worst doing, will remain one. Redemption is about us recognizing our embeddedness in the world, acknowledging our striving to deepen this embeddedness, and finding the courage to forge the relations and practices that allow this embeddedness to evolve, flourish, and blossom.

VIII

The Walls of the Bible

The Bible speaks compellingly about matters of space and design. In many instances, the Bible associates walls with fragmentation and separation. Walls are consistently discussed in relation to aggression, domination, isolation, and expansion. We find many instances in the Old Testament where God is directing different peoples to build walls. Walls even surround Jerusalem, the holy city. It is supposedly the obligation of God's chosen peoples to build great walls so as to protect themselves against the world's ungodly peoples. Indeed, most walls in the Bible seem to have the blessings of God. But how could this possibly be so? Walls, after all, undermine the expansion of our humanity by limiting our interaction with peoples of different realities and experiences. Moreover, walls make us impermeable and inflexible by keeping us beholden to one reality. They block the evolution of new and different ways of experiencing and understanding the world. That is, in undermining diversity walls undermine life's evolution.

Deuteronomy 1: 27-29

You grumbled in your tents and said, "The LORD hates us; so he brought us out of Egypt to deliver us into the hands of the Amorites to destroy us.

Where can we go? Our brothers have made us lose heart. They say, 'The people are stronger and taller than we are; the cities are large, with walls up to the sky. We even saw the Anakites there.'"

Then I said to you, "Do not be terrified; do not be afraid of them.

Deuteronomy 3: 1-6

Next we turned and went up along the road toward Bashan, and Og king of Bashan with his whole army marched out to meet us in battle at Edrei.

The LORD said to me, "Do not be afraid of him, for I have handed him over to you with his whole army and his land. Do to him what you did to Sihon king of the Amorites, who reigned in Heshbon."

So the LORD our God also gave into our hands Og king of Bashan and all his army. We struck them down, leaving no survivors.

At that time we took all his cities. There was not one of the sixty cities that we did not take from them--the whole region of Argob, Og's kingdom in Bashan.

All these cities were fortified with high walls and with gates and bars, and there were also a great many unwalled villages.
We completely destroyed them, as we had done with Sihon king of Heshbon, destroying every city--men, women and children.

Deuteronomy 9: 1-2

Hear, O Israel. You are now about to cross the Jordan to go in and dispossess nations greater and stronger than you, with large cities that have walls up to the sky.

The people are strong and tall--Anakites! You know about them and have heard it said: "Who can stand up against the Anakites?"

Deuteronomy 28: 51-53

They will devour the young of your livestock and the crops of your land until you are destroyed. They will leave you no grain, new wine or oil, nor any calves of your herds or lambs of your flocks until you are ruined.

They will lay siege to all the cities throughout your land until the high fortified walls in which you trust fall down. They will besiege all the cities throughout the land the LORD your God is giving you.

Because of the suffering that your enemy will inflict on you during the siege, you will eat the fruit of the womb, the flesh of the sons and daughters the LORD your God has given you.

Micah 7: 10-12

Then my enemy will see it and will be covered with shame, she who said to me, "Where is the LORD your God?" My eyes will see her downfall; even now she will be trampled underfoot like mire in the streets.

The day for building your walls will come, the day for extending your boundaries.

In that day people will come to you from Assyria and the cities of Egypt, even from Egypt to the Euphrates and from sea to sea and from mountain to mountain.

We do find one instance, however, in Ezekiel, where the absence of walls characterizes a peaceful and trusting people.

Ezekiel 38: 10-12

This is what the Sovereign LORD says: On that day thoughts will come into your mind and you will devise an evil scheme.

You will say, "I will invade a land of unwalled villages; I will attack a peaceful and unsuspecting people—all of them living without walls and without gates and bars.

I will plunder and loot and turn my hand against the resettled ruins and the people gathered from the nations, rich in livestock and goods, living at the center of the land."

But why is God apparently encouraging and ordaining a relation to space and place that brings nothing but aggression and destruction? Even today, the walls, temples, mosques, synagogues, and churches that God supposedly directs us to build threaten to plunge the world into the war that will end all wars. Arguably, no other spaces and places separate and fragment us more than our different temples, mosques, synagogues, and churches. They help us make believe that our Gods are *really* different. Our religious and spiritual differences therefore appear to be intractable and irreconcilable. Indeed, what more of a difference can be found between people than different Gods? What difference can foster more loyalty and, consequently, more separation and fragmentation? Such a difference makes believe that we have—and will never really have—no common humanity. We are therefore released of any obligation to find union and communion with persons of different faiths and religions. We are spared of risking life. We can believe that we are entitled to our different religions, and that we have no moral foundation upon which to challenge each other's moral practices. Indeed, we have generally agreed that a civil society promotes religious toleration. Yet this kind of toleration inadvertently promotes separation and fragmentation by reifying the differences between religions.

To focus on the religious practices rather than the spiritual teachings that identify different peoples is to miss how, in most cases, religious practices are merely caricatures of spiritual teachings. In too many cases, unfortunately, such practices tend to obfuscate our common humanness and humanity. In this regard, our different mosques, synagogues, temples, and churches work well for us. To believe that our Gods are different releases us of any moral and spiritual obligation to forge union and communion with others who appear most different to us by sparing us from the tribulations and threats to our own life that come with such obligations.

To believe that we are of different Gods therefore separates us physically, morally, and spiritually. There is arguably no other difference that separates and fragments us more. Consequently, this difference poses the most perilous threat to our redemption and salvation. What makes this difference such a threat is that our different actions are seen to have the authority and blessings of our Gods. God supposedly legitimizes our waging of war upon others, our slaughtering of innocent people, our killing of our sisters for adulterous affairs, our beheading of persons for various immoral acts, our ordering the execution of other persons for writing blasphemous verses, and other such heinous religious practices. We are, in the end, merely doing God's work. To believe our Gods are different gives our cowardice religious legitimacy.

Yet all the spiritual teachings that inform the world's great religions stress union and communion. We also find in these teachings the notion that God resides between our relations with each other. Our relationships are our houses of worship. Through our relationships we worship, experience, and understand God. But, of course, these houses of worship are much more difficult to build and sustain than physical houses of worship. So we have decided instead to build physical, rather than spiritual, houses of worship. But at what cost? All spiritual teachings stress again and again that our redemption resides in the evolution and expansion of our humanity, which only comes with our willingness to love deeply and selflessly. No teaching gives us a way out of this reality. As such, no person or group can claim any moral or spiritual legitimacy in the use of violence to protect any place or space.

The Gospels of Matthew, Mark, Luke, and John

Interestingly, no mention of walls is found in the gospels of Matthew, Mark, Luke, and John. Jesus Christ never encourages or ordains the building of walls. In fact, Jesus Christ never calls for the construction of any kind of religious building. In my view, the absence of direction by Jesus Christ for his followers to build walls, temples, mosques, and churches is by no means arbitrary. It was deliberate. Jesus Christ, according to the New Testament, brings the New Covenant—the covenant of union. This covenant stresses communion rather subordination to God. It is against aggression, military expansion, domination, and other such actions. This New Covenant calls us to love others deeply and selflessly, especially those who trespass against us by destroying and defacing our holy spaces and places. In fact, we have to love both the just and the unjust. Discrimination is never an option. Thus our spaces and designs must help foster love and compassion for those who are most different to us, which explains why Jesus Christ was always in dialogue with persons of different spiritual and moral persuasions.

The New Testament makes no mention of Jesus Christ calling for the building of physical houses of worship. Instead, Jesus Christ calls us to go into the world and into the spaces of the poor, downtrodden, oppressed, and marginalized; the reason being that our own redemption is intertwined with the plight of the poor, downtrodden, oppressed, and marginalized. The New Testament reminds us that we are biologically, ecologically, and spiritually bound together. We are spiritually obligated to transgress those spaces and designs that promote fragmentation and separation. Thus, in challenging us to love deeply and selflessly, Jesus Christ gives us a gospel that rejects spaces and designs that promote fragmentation and separation. Only those spaces and places that promote union and communion are holy and sacred.

Our fighting and killing of each other over different physical structures is simply contrary to the ways of any God that stresses love and compassion. Yet, to believe that our houses of God are holy poses no threat to the status quo. This belief releases us of any commitment to construct new and different ways of being in the world. To believe in the notion of houses of worship merely requires obedient submission. We supposedly do well with God by consistently and diligently going to our temples, mosques, and churches and by being committed to the upkeep of these buildings. In too many cases, our relation to God is reduced to a relation to a building. What matters is our submission to this building. We have excised the human element. Our relation to God is mediated by our relation to a building. The New Covenant ends this kind of mediation. It foregrounds the human element. Our relation to God is now mediated by our relation to each other. The result is a different relation to God.

Jesus Christ's own life speaks of a person trying to love deeply and selflessly. This is the New Covenant between God and us. To love deeply and selflessly is to commit ourselves to fostering ways of being that promote union and communion. Thus, Jesus Christ pushes us to focus on whether our design ecology is deepening our ability to love deeply and selflessly. He challenges us to reconceptualize our spaces and designs in order to address more sacred concerns. He brings a moral dimension to the organization of our spaces. In this way, Jesus Christ politicizes our spaces and designs by discouraging the formation of those spaces and designs that foster fear, suspicion, and apathy.

New Gods and Straight Lines

There must be something to the fact that there are no perfectly straight lines in the natural world. Yet such lines permeate our own worlds. Such lines represent order for us. They supposedly represent our power over nature—our bringing order to a supposedly chaotic and disorderly world. They also supposedly show us bringing perfection to an imperfect world. In other words, straight lines show us that we have the ability to attain perfection, to transcend our imperfect humanity, to conquer the world. This is why straight lines characterize fascism, fundamentalism, and modernism. We would have no capitalism or socialism without straight lines. Straight lines reflect our deepest anxieties. Yet, on the other hand, such lines also aptly capture our separation and alienation from the natural world.

> *Modernism did its immense damage in these ways: by divorcing the practice of building from the history and traditional meanings of building; by promoting a species of urbanism that destroyed age-old social arrangements and, with them, urban life as a general proposition; and by creating a physical setting for man that failed to respect the limits of scale, growth, and the consumption of natural resources, or to respect the lives of other living things. The result of Modernism, especially in America, is a crisis of the human habitat: cities ruined by corporate gigantism and abstract renewal schemes, public buildings and public spaces unworthy of human affection, vast sprawling suburbs that lack any sense of community, housing that the un-rich cannot afford to live in, a slavish obedience to the needs of automobiles and their dependent industries at the expense of human needs, and a gathering ecological calamity that we have only begun to measure.*
>
> James   Howard   Kunstler,
> *The Geography of Nowhere*

Perfection is purely a human construct. It has no origin or purchase in the natural world. In fact, perfection is death in the natural world. Nothing in the natural world is inherently perfect—that is, without defects, flaws, deficiencies, and shortcomings. It is these supposed imperfections, however, that make evolution possible. Without these supposed imperfections, evolution would end and life would stop. As such, perfection—or the questing for perfection—promotes death. It represents us waging war upon the natural world. Worse of all, perfection is about illusions. The natural world would never allow us to achieve perfection. It is ontologically impossible. It would represent the end of life. Imperfection is therefore status quo in the natural world.

Yet perfection consumes us. Our fixation with attaining perfect bodies, creating perfect foods, finding the perfect mate, making perfect babies, creating perfect societies, is everywhere. In fact, we have long been consumed with perfection, as can be seen in our never-ending quest to create the perfect race. The great promise of modernity has always been perfection—a world without pain, sickness, chaos, misery, and even death. How could such a world be forsaken? On the other hand, how did we come to desire such a world to begin with? How did chaos, suffering, pain, and so forth come to make for an undesirable and imperfect world? When did we begin to find imperfection in the natural world? How did our pursuit of illusions begin? How could we possibly believe that we can conquer life? But we do, and there is no letting up in our quest to do so.

Of course no one wants to believe that we have anything in common with fascists. Even to mention us in the same breath with fascists is sacrilegious. But we are of the same ideological and cosmological orientation as fascists. What distinguishes us is merely honesty. But, we too believe that society's ills result from our imperfections, we too believe that our architectural infrastructure should be used to bring order and perfection to our societies, and we too believe in the employment of science to help bring perfection to an inherently imperfect world. Ultimately, for all its cultural sophistication, modernity makes it impossible to be anything but a fascist, and what passes for postmodernism is merely a desperate reaction to the harsh realities of modernism. In fact, nothing in postmodernism is really postmodern. We have never been disabused of our quest for perfection. Even in postmodernism, straight lines are status quo. Then again postmodernism was never meant as a revolution. It was always shot through with modernism. Contrary to public perception, it was always meant to help sustain the hegemony of modernism. After all, one cannot have a revolution that begins and ends with negation.

But now we are beyond both modernism and postmodernism. We are now in the throes of supermodernism. Supermodernism is modernism without reservations. In supermodernism, the straight line is more than ideological, it is cosmological. There is no truth, no reality, no redemption, outside of the straight line. Only straight lines sustain life and make for civility and progress. Supermodernism aims to use straight lines to order the world. It also seeks to assimilate cultures and societies that forward other kinds of lines. Moreover, supermodernism strives for an unsurpassed perfection. It believes that this perfection is necessary for our prosperity. Also, supermodernism believes that achieving this perfect perfection is necessary to show that *man* (literally) is god, which is to say that *man* has more than the ability to order the world: he actually possesses the ability—through science—to be the master of the world. Thus, whereas the best any god could do is to create an imperfect world, *man*, in achieving perfect perfection, shows that he is beyond the power of any god and, for certain, beyond being any god's humble servant. In short, supermodernism is about *man* as god. God is finally dead. Long live the reign of *man*.

Supermodernism believes that modern science is our greatest expression. It is through modern science, after all, that we have gone from mere mortals to great gods. The arts and humanities have supposedly played no fundamental role in this elevation. Supermodernism chastises the arts and humanities for wanting us to believe that we should be content with being mere fragile and imperfect mortals. As such, supermodernism is committed to the propagation of modern science. It is determined to have modern science control each and every facet of our lives.

Supermodernism is born out of the fact that we have never been disabused of the need for perfection. After all, what is inherently wrong with perfection? Even if perfection is theoretically unattainable, what is wrong with at least questing for perfection? Why should we settle for imperfect foods, imperfect bodies, imperfect mates, imperfect children, imperfect societies, and imperfect worlds, especially when science can supposedly and presumably spare us these imperfections that do nothing good for us? What is inherently wrong with straight lines? On the other hand, what is inherently heuristic about non-straight lines? Moreover, though perfection may have no purchase in the natural world, this in no way means that it has no purchase in our social, cultural, and political worlds. So what exactly is the case against perfection?

The case can be found in any of the spiritual texts that guide the world's great religions. In none of these texts do we find perfection being related to our redemption. In fact, in all of these texts we find imperfect gods and imperfect prophets. Also, none of these texts demand perfection from us. Instead, they require us to care more, give more, love more, empathize more, forgive more, and so forth. The reason being, I believe, is that such doing continuously enlarges our being and, in so doing, pushes us to new realms of being. Perfection is stasis. Even if we could attain perfection, or some semblance of perfection, what would be next? How would we create and sustain meaning in a perfect world? Where would meaning come from? What would catalyze meaning creation? In short, perfection does nothing for us. It keeps us fixated with the material and the physical, and, though such a fixation probably has uses, it also has serious limitations—which, again, explains why all the world's great spiritual texts warn us against it. One reason being the physical is always subject to meaning. That is, no physical condition has any inherent meaning. For instance, my lack of hearing can mean something completely different to me than what it means to the next person. So the physical has no power to name its own condition. Moreover, in being inherently unstable, all meanings are subject to change. Thus, why be fixated with something that has neither power nor agency? It would seem that we would be much better off concerning ourselves with where meaning resides and with those practices that generate and shape meaning. In such a case we would have to focus on the nonphysical realms, as meaning comes from the center of our being.

Enter trust, compassion, hope, faith, forgiveness, and mercy. These practices expand meaning creation and, accordingly, expand our humanity. These practices are in no way merely religious and arbitrary practices. They are integral to making us fully human and, in so doing, allowing us to escape a world laden with the bestiality that inevitably comes with being less human. As such, even Jacques Derrida now writes about the need for forgiveness in an increasingly cosmopolitan world.

To focus on meaning creation is to realize that our redemption is intertwined with our becoming human and has nothing to do with perfection. We also realize that what being human demands of us is different than what perfection demands of us. In fact, we realize that the demands of perfection conflict with those being human. Perfection, for instance, requires the ending of complexity and ambiguity. We must be able to exercise complete and absolute control so as to avoid the entry of unplanned variables and thereby unplanned outcomes—that is, imperfect outcomes. Nothing must be unforeseen. Perfection therefore requires us to believe that we can actually impose our will on the world. But the challenge of being human makes no such impossible demands on us. To end complexity and ambiguity, or at least to be committed to doing so, undermines the conditions that most heighten meaning creation. In other words, meaning creation evolves towards complexity and ambiguity. As our capacity to generate meanings enlarges, the meanings that emerge from us are more and more complex and ambiguous; which is to say that such meanings are more interpretive, narrative, and expansive.

Such are the meanings that make for a world with less war, misery, suffering, and all kinds of strife. That is, such are the meanings that save us from damnation. Also, as our meanings become more interpretive, narrative, and expansive, we become more in harmony with the quantum rhythms and tensions that constitute the world. We lose our fear of the world's supposedly negative forces, such as discontinuity, instability, and ambiguity. We come to recognize the inherent virtues of an incomplete world—one that will lend itself to neither one Truth nor one God. We are thereby released of the need for complete Truths, as well as the accompanying tendency to impose such Truths (and Gods) on others who claim different truths. Perfection is therefore a hallmark of moral retardation. It speaks to an inability to recognize the world's infinite complexity and ambiguity—that is, the world's inherent beauty. This is why perfection will always surround the worse expressions of being human.

But there are other problems that come with straight lines. Such lines limit design by limiting innovation and imagination. After all, straight lines can only go, well, straight; either straight up or straight across. To base designs on such lines therefore requires that we maintain a limited point of reference and, even worse, forces us to maintain such a point of reference. The results are predictable and indistinguishable designs. Indeed, how much imagination is involved in designing those tall boxes that define modern architecture? Architects, for sure, often contend that they are merely responding to the needs of clients for efficient and cost effective buildings. But straight lines define all realms of modern architecture.

The hegemony of these lines cannot be divorced from a worldview that limits innovation and imagination by discouraging the evolution of new ways of experiencing and understanding the world. That is, the hegemony of straight lines compellingly speaks to the lack of imagination that comes with moral retardation. Imagination and moral development are intertwined. That we make no such connection, much less notice our own limited imagination, is because we are still of a worldview that encourages us to view the world in pieces rather than in wholes. Moreover, this worldview prescribes that we look at the world as a machine, that buildings function as machines, and that such buildings make our societies function like efficient machines. Le Corbusier, for instance, who was arguably one of the most influential architectural theorists of the twentieth century, was adamant about designs as machines. Further, straight lines accentuate the mental and cognitive dimensions of being human; which is to say that such lines make for designs that are inherently (supposedly) rational, pushing persons who inhabit these designs to act this way. We achieve this rationality through a redundancy of walls and right-angles, and through huge abstract and rigid buildings that overwhelm and dwarf us. In short, straight lines physically afford the construction of a society that allows for the most control—a control that is necessary because our society rests on a worldview that conspires in every way to keep us less human.

Frank Gehry's design of the Guggenheim Museum in Bilbao, Spain, is without a doubt one of the most defining buildings of our time. The building curves everywhere. It is very voluptuous. Gehry claims that the design was only possible because of new design technology that facilitates curvy designs. He is partially correct. Bilbao also reflects the fact that we are in the midst of a paradigm shift. We are ready for voluptuous and sensuous buildings. We are less and less afraid of the world's sensuality. We are beginning to find the courage to imagine the world in bold new ways. This is what Gehry's Bilbao captures. It also captures the fact that the machine metaphor no longer works for us. We no longer believe the world has no soul, no life, no passion. The challenge we face now is finding designs that complement this world we are now realizing. Such designs, for sure, will be devoid of straight lines. They will show no defiance of the world's quantum tensions, and stand as no testament of our success in conquering an inherently chaotic and imperfect world. They will therefore be more sensual than mechanical, more organic than inorganic, more emergent than imposed.

Epilogue

Michael Foucault contends that "A whole history remains to be written of spaces—which would at the same time be the history of power—from the great strategies of geopolitics to the little tactics of the habitat." I would add that what also needs to be written is a history that focuses on the impact of different spaces and designs on the human condition. The impact, for sure, has been tremendous.

Because of the physical nature of our spaces and designs, they have the ability to exert the most influence on us in shaping our understanding of the world and ourselves. More importantly, they have the ability—gain because of their physical nature—to have the most enduring influence. Thus, even when we are ready to look at the world differently, our spatial infrastructure works to sustain the status quo. Further, our spatial infrastructure is in no way sustained purely by its physical nature. It is interlocked with other ideological, political, legal, social, and cultural infrastructures, such as property laws, building codes, zoning laws, national policies, and so forth. All of these infrastructures work in tandem to maintain the status quo. For instance, recently the Supreme Court unanimously decided to give cities and communities a new legal tool to privatize public spaces. Don Mitchell (2003) of Syracuse University contends that this new tool "is perhaps the most powerful tool of all, since it allows government agencies themselves to make what is public—and so ours as citizens, over which we have rights—fully private. With this privatization we won't so much be citizens as potential trespassers on what ought to be collective, public spaces, the very kind of spaces that give a city its vitality."

Other trends portend nothing good for us. We continue to separate and fragment. Walls and fences are going up everywhere. Ariel Sharon even has the audacity to say that that Israel's new border fence will promote friendship.

Yet the evolution of new spaces and designs cannot come before, or be separated from, the evolution of a worldview that promotes union rather than fragmentation. Fortunately for us, such a worldview is now upon us, and we are slowly beginning to imagine new spaces and designs.

The primary goal of this book was to show the inseparable relationship between how we understand the world and how we physically and spatially layout the world. The fact that our spaces and designs continue to fragment us, and that we continue to believe that walls and fences can keep us safe, only shows that we are yet to have any meaningful appreciation of the human costs of our present approach to our spaces and designs.

But there is hope. Hope in the fact that more and more people are writing about the impact of our current spaces and designs. Hope also in the fact that more and more people are expressing desire for community rather than suburban homes. Hope also in the fact that our collapsing distances and spaces is pushing us to recognize that we are really of one place. Ultimately, we have to find a way to more than simply coexist in this one place; we have to find communion in this one place. Theoretically, this communion is possible. It is within our potentiality. We can do this. We have to be always striving for this communion. There is simply no other path to life.

References

Anderson, R., Cissna, K. N., & Arnett, R. C. (1994). Communication and the ground for dialogue. In R. Anderson, K. Cissna, & R. Arnett (Eds.), *The reach of dialogue: Confirmation, voice, and community* (pp. 9-30). Cresskill, NJ: Hampton.

Arnett, R. (1986). *Communication and community.* Carbondale, IL: Southern Illinois University.

Arnett, R. C. (1994). Existential homeless: A contemporary case for dialogue. In R. Anderson, K. Cissna, & R. Arnett (Eds.), *The reach of dialogue: Confirmation, voice, and community* (pp. 229-246). Cresskill, NJ: Hampton.

Bachelard, G. (1964). *The poetics of space.* Boston: Beacon Press.

Boal, F. W. (1978). Ethnic residential segregation. In D. T. Herbert & R. J. Johnston (Eds.) *Social areas in cities: Processes, patterns and problems: Vol. 1. Spatial Processes and Form (pp. 57-95).* Chichester, UK: Wiley.

Boger, J. C., & Wgner, J. W. (Eds.) (1996). *Race, poverty, and American cities.* Chapel Hill, NC: The University of North Carolina Press.

Bohm, D. (1996). *On dialogue.* New York. Routledge.

Bullard, R. D., Grigsby, E. III, & Lee C. (Eds.)(1994). *Residential apartheid: The American legacy.* Los Angeles: Center for Afro-American Studies, University of California at Los Angeles.

Buber, M. (1994). Genuine dialogue and the possibilities of peace. In R. Anderson, K. Cissna, & R. Arnett (Eds.), *The reach of dialogue: Confirmation, voice, and community* (pp. 306-312). Cresskill, NJ: Hampton.

Caldiera, T.P.R. (1996). Fortified enclaves: The new urban segregation. *Public Culture, 8,* 303-328.

Calmore, J. O. (1996). Spatial equality and the Kerner Commission report. In J. C. Boger, & J. W. Wagner (Eds.), *Race, poverty, and American cities* (pp. 309-342). Chapel Hill, NC: University of North Carolina Press.

Castells, M. (1997). *The information age: Economy, society and culture v.ii: The power of identity*. Malden, MA: Blackwell.

Castells, M. (1998). *The information age: Economy, society and culture v.iii: End of millennium*. Malden, MA: Blackwell.

Castells, M. (2000). *The information age: Economy, society and culture v.i: The rise of the network society (second edition)*. Malden, MA: Blackwell.

Cissna, K. N., & Anderson, R. (1994). Communication and the ground of dialogue. In R. Anderson, K. Cissna, & R. Arnett (Eds.), *The reach of dialogue: Confirmation, voice, and community* (pp. 9-30). Cresskill, NJ: Hampton.

Cook, R. (1997, May 24). Suburbia: Land of varied faces and a growing political force. *Congressional Quarterly Weekly Report*, pp. 1209-1217.

Cronen, V. E. (1998). Communication theory for the twenty-first century: Cleaning up the wreckage of the psychology project. In J. S. Trent (Ed.), *Communication: Views from the helm for the twenty-first century* (pp. 18-38). New York: Allyn & Bacon.

Cutler, D.M., Glaeser, E.L., & Vigdor, J.L. (1999). The rise and decline of the American ghetto. *Journal of Political Economy, 107*, 455-506.

Dawkins, R. (1989). *The selfish gene*. Oxford: Oxford University Press.

Downs, A. (1998). The big picture: How American cities are growing. *Brookings Review, 16*, 8-11.

Dreier, P., & Moberg, D. (1996, Winter). Moving from the hood: The mixed success of integrating suburbia. *The American Prospect*, pp. 1-9.

Dreier, P. (1996). America's urban crisis: Symptoms, causes, and solutions. In J. C. Boger, & J. W. Wgner (Eds.), *Race, Poverty, and American Cities* (pp. 79-142). Chapel Hill, NC: University of North Carolina Press.

Duany, A., Plater-Zyberk, E., & Speck, J. (2000). *Suburban nation: The rise of sprawl and the decline of the American dream*. Berkeley, CA: North Point.

Farley, F. E. (1995). Race still matters. *Urban Affairs Review, 31*, 244-254.

Fischer, C. S., Hout, M., Jankowski, M. S., Lucas, S. R., Swidler, A., & Voss, K. (1996). *Inequality by design: Cracking the bell curve myth*. Princeton, NJ: Princeton University Press.

Flynn, R. L. (1995). America's cities: Centers of culture, commerce, and community. *Urban Affairs Review*, 30, 635-640.

Freire, P. (1993). *Pedagogy of the oppressed*. New York: Continuum.

Fromm, E. (1956). *The art of loving*. New York: Harper & Row.

Fromm, E. (1973). *The anatomy of human destructiveness*. New York: Henry Holt.

Garreau, J. (1991). *Edge city: Life on the new frontier*. New York: Doubleday.

Gilder, G.F. (1981). *Wealth and poverty*. New York: Basic Books.

Goldberger, P. (2000, March 27). Solving suburban sprawl. *New Yorker*, 28-129.

Goldsmith, W., & Blakely, E. (1992). *Separate societies: Poverty and inequality in U.S. cities*. Philadelphia: Temple University Press.

Goodman, E. (1994, November 13). Haves, have-nots now coldly judged as winners, losers. *Los Angeles Times*, p. 5.

Grosz, E. (2001). *Architecture from the outside*. Cambridge, MA: MIT Press.

Harvey, D. (1990). *The condition of postmodernity*. Cambridge, MA: Blackwell.

Harvey, D. (2000). *Spaces of hope*. Berkeley, CA: University of California Press.

Herrnstein, R. J., & Murray, C. (1994). *The Bell Curve: Intelligence and class structure in American life*. New York: Free Press.

Hwang, S., Murdoch, S. T. (1998). Racial attraction or racial avoidance in American suburbs? *Social Forces, 77*, 541-566.

Ibelings, H. (1998). *Supermodernism: Architecture in the age of globalization*. Rotterdam: NAI.

Iyer, P. (2000). *The global soul: Jet lag, shopping malls, and the search for home*. New York: Knopf.

Jackson, K. T. (1985). *Crabgrass frontier: The suburbanization of the United States*. New York: Oxford University Press.

Jameson, F. (1991). *Postmodernism or the cultural logic of late capitalism*. Durham, NC: Duke University Press.

Jencks, C. (1997). *The architecture of the jumping universe*. New York: Academy Editions.

Jencks, C. (1991). Is the American underclass growing? In C. Jencks & P. E. Petersen (Eds.), *The urban underclass*. Washington, DC: Brookings Institution.

Jencks, C. (1977). *The language of post-modern architecture*. New York: Rizzoli.

Judd, D. R. (1995). The new walled cities. In H. Liggett & D. C. Perry (Eds.), *Spatial practices: Critical explorations in social/spatial theory*. Thousand Oaks, CA: Sage.

Katznelson, I. (2002, Winter). Evil & politics. *Daedalus*, pp. 7-10.

Keating, D. (1994). *The suburban dilemma*. Philadelphia: Temple University Press.

Kozol, J. (1992). *Savage inequalities: Children in America's schools*. New York: HarperPerennial.

Kunstler, J. H. (1993). *The geography of nowhere*. New York: Touchstone.

Lasch, C. (1984). *The minimal self*. New York: W. W. Norton.

Lehrer, E. (1998, November 1). Burbsprawl: Room to be Free? *Insight On The News*, 18-20. Liebmann, G. (1999, November/December). A Republican agenda for the suburbs. *The American Enterprise*, 68-69.

Liggett, H., & Perry, D. C. (Eds.) (1995). *Spatial practices: Critical explorations in social/spatial theory*. Thousand Oaks, CA: Sage.

Liska, A. E., Logan, J. R. Logan, & Bellair, P. E. (1998). Race and violent crime in the suburbs. *American Sociological Review, 63*, 27-38.

Longman, P. J. (1998, April 27). Who pays for sprawl? *U.S. News & World Report*, 22-24.

Marcuse, P. (1994). Not chaos but walls: Postmodernism and partitioned city. In S. Watson & K.Gibson (Eds.), *Postmodern cities and spaces*. Oxford, UK: Basil Blackwell.

Marcuse, P. (1996). Space and race in the post-Fordist city: The outcast ghetto and advanced homelessness in the United States today. In E. Mingione (Ed.), *Urban poverty and the underclass*. Oxford, UK: Basil Blackwell.

Marcuse, P. (1997a). The enclave, the citadel, and the ghetto: What has changed in the post-Fordist U.S. city? *Urban Affairs Review, 33*, 228-264.

Marcuse, P. (1997b). Walls of fear and walls of support. In N. Ellin (Ed.), *Architecture of Fear* (pp. 104-114). Princeton, NJ: Princeton University Press.

Marcuse, P. (1997c). The ghetto of exclusion and the fortified enclave: New patterns in the United States. *The American Behavioral Scientist, 41*, 311-326.

Massey, D. S., & Denton, N. A. (1993). *American apartheid: Segregation and the making of the underclass*. Cambridge, MA: Harvard University Press.

McClain, P. D. (1995). Thirty years of urban policies: Frankly, my dears, we don't give a damn! *Urban Affairs Review, 30*, 641-644.

McNamee, S., & Gergen, K. J. (1999). *Relational responsibility: Resources for sustainable dialogue*. Thousand Oaks, CA: Sage.

Merton, T. (1967). *No man is an island*. New York: Doubleday.

Mingione, E. (Ed.). (1996). *Urban poverty and the underclass*. Oxford, UK: Basil Blackwell.

Morales, E. (2002). *Living in Spanglish: The search for Latino identity in America*. New York: St. Martin's Griffin.

Musante, F. (1998, January 4). Databases are building for political shifts of 2002. *The New York Times*, CN1-4.

Norval, M. (2002, March). Terrorism and globalization. *Chronicles*, pp. 20-22.

O'Meara, M. (1999, July/August). U.S. voters tell suburbia to slow down. *World Watch, 9*. Patterson, O. (1999, April 30). When "They" are "Us." *The New York Times*.

Patterson, O. (1997). *The ordeal of integration: Progress and resentment in America's racial crisis*. Washington, D.C.: Civitas/Counterpoint.

Phelan, T.J., & Schneider, M. (1996). Race, ethnicity, and suburbs in American suburbs. Urban *Affairs Review, 31*, 659-680.

Putnam, R. (2000). *Bowling alone: The collapse and revival of American community*. New York: Simon & Schuster.

Rodriguez, A. (2002a). Culture to culturing: Re-imagining our understanding of intercultural relations. *Intercultural Communication, 5*. http://www.immi.se/intercultural/.

Rodriguez, A. J. (2003). *Diversity as liberation (II): Introducing a new understanding of diversity*. Cresskill, NJ: Hampton.

Rodriguez, R. (2002b). *Brown: The last discovery of America.* New York: Penguin.

Ross, S. (2000, September 22). On racism, we've still a long way to go, report finds. *Journal and Courier,* p. A. 4.

Salins, P. D. (1997). *Assimilation American style.* New York: Basic Books.

Sen, A. (2000, July). East and west: The reach of reason. *New York Book Review* (On line edition).

Soja, E. W. (1989). *Postmodern geographies.* New York: Verso Press.

South, S. J., & Crowder, K. D. (1998). Leaving the hood: Residential mobility between black, white, and integrated neighborhoods. *American Sociological Review, 63,* 17-26.

Southworth, M., & Ben-Joseph, B. (1997). *Streets and the shaping of towns and cities.* New York: McGraw-Hill.

Sowell, T. (1994). *Race and culture.* New York: Basic Books.

Stoesz, D. (1996). Poor policy: The legacy of the Kerner Commission for social welfare. In J. C. Boger, & J. W. Wagner (Eds.), *Race, poverty, and American cities* (pp. 309-342). Chapel Hill, NC: University of North Carolina Press.

Sugrue, T. J. (1996). *The origins of the urban crisis: Race and inequality in postwar Detroit.* Princeton, NJ: Princeton University Press.

Thomas, G.S. (1995). America's most educated places. *American Demographics, 17,* 44-51.

Van Dijk, J. A. G. M. (2002). *The one dimensional network society of Manuel Castells.* http://www.thechronicle.demon.co.uk/archive/castells.htm.

Venturi, R., Brown, D. S., & Izenour, S. (1977). *Learning from Las Vegas.* Cambridge, MA: MIT Press.

Wacquant, L. (1993). Urban outcasts: Stigma and division. *International Journal of Urban and Regional, 17,* 366-383.

Weisman, L. K. (1992). *Discrimination by design: A feminist critique of the man-made environment.* Chicago: University of Illinois Press.

West, C. (1993). *Race matters.* Boston: Beacon Press.

Will, G. (1995, April 24). What's behind income disparity. *San Francisco Chronicle,* A15.

Wilson, W. J. (1987). *The truly disadvantaged: The inner city, the underclass, and public policy.* Chicago: University of Chicago Press.

Wilson, W. J. (1991). Studying inner-city social dislocations: The challenge of public agenda research. *American Sociological Review, 56,* 6.

Wilson, E. O. (1978). *On human nature.* Cambridge, MA: Harvard University Press.

Wright, R. (1994). *The moral animal: The new science of evolutionary psychology.* New York: Vintage.

Wright, W. (1998). *Born that way: Genes, behavior, personality.* New York: Knopf.

Index

alienation , 8, 10, 34, 73, 80
Anderson, R. , 7, 17, 18 , 88
Arnett, R. , 8, 17, 34 , 88
Bachelard, G. , 13
Boal, F. W. , 2
Boger, J. C. , 2 , 88
Bohm, D. , 19, 20, 21, 60, 62, 63
Buber, M. , 7, 17, 18
Bullard, R. D. , 2, 34
Caldiera, T. , 2
Calmore, J. O. , 2, 4
capitalism , 6, 7, 22, 31, 32, 71, 80
Castells, M. , 13, 22, 23, 24
Chakrabarty, D. , 36
Cissna, K. N. , 7, 17, 18
citadels , 3
community , 1, 2, 9, 28, 29, 30, 31, 33,
    34, 35, 38, 39, 44, 50, 58, 60, 80, 86
compassion, viii, 17, 18, 19, 14, 33, 34,
    37, 68, 71, 72, 78, 79, 82
Cook, R. , 2, 3
crisis of communication , 7
Cronen, V. E. , 16
culture of survivalism , 8
Cutler, D. M. , 2, 34
Dawkins, R.
democracy , vii, 2, 56
dialogue , 17, 18, 19, 20, 21, 24, 34, 42,
    48, 62, 78
Downs, A. , 2
Dreier, P. , 2, 3, 4
Duany, A. , 1, 2, 5, 9

Farley, F. E. , 2, 4
Fischer, C. S. , 10
Flynn, R. L. , 2
fragmentation , 2, 5, 6, 7, 9, 10, 11, 18,
    19, 20, 21, 24, 33, 34, 48, 49, 50,
    58, 61, 67, 73, 75, 77, 79, 86
Freire, P. , 18, 21
Fromm, E. , 8, 33
Garreau, J. , 2
ghettoization , 3
Gilder, G. F. , 7
Goldberger, P. , 1
Goldsmith, W. , 1, 3
good society , 6, 7, 14, 36, 37, 71
Goodman, E. , 5
Grosz, E. , 13
Harvey, D. , 13
hegemony , 2, 43, 46, 61, 71, 81, 83
Herrnstein, R. J. , 7
Huntington, S., 28
Hwang, S. , 2
Ibelings, H. , 14, 24, 25
Iyer, P. , 41, 44, 45, 46
Jackson, K. T. , 5
Jameson, F. , 13
Jencks, C. , 3, 13, 14, 20, 21, 24
Judd, D. R. , 3
Katznelson, I. , 31, 32, 35, 36, 37, 38
Keating, D. , 2
Kozol, J. , 10
Kunstler, J. H. , 2, 80
Lasch, C. , 8

Lehrer, E. , 4, 5
liberalism , 7, 31, 32, 35, 36, 37, 38
Liggett, H. , 1, 2
Liska, A. E. , 2
Logan, J. R. , 2
Longman, P. J. , 4, 5
Marcuse, P. , 2, 3, 4
market forces , 6
Massey, D. S. , 1, 3, 4, 5
McClain, P. D. , 3, 4
McNamee, S. , 8
Merton, T. , 1
Mingione, E. , 3, 4
Morales, E. , 41, 42, 43, 44, 49, 50, 51
multicultural , 28, 29, 31, 33, 39, 43, 49, 51
Musante, F. , 4
nationhood , 2
Norval, M. , 28
Patterson, O. , 10
Phelan, T. J. , 1, 3
politics of homicide , 4
Putnam, R. , 34, 35
rationality , 35, 36, 37, 83
Rodriguez, A. J. , 7, 42
Rodriguez, R. , 45, 48, 50, 51

Ronald Reagan , 4
Ross, S. , 2
Salins, P. D. , 31, 32
Sen, A. , 29, 37
Soja, E. W. , 13, 14
South, S. J. , 2
Southworth, M. , 1, 2, 3, 9
Sowell, T. , 6, 7
Spanglish , vi, 41, 43, 45, 46, 47, 48, 49, 50, 51
Stoesz, D. , 1, 3, 4
Sugrue, T. J. , 3
supermodernism , 25, 81
Ten Commandments , 11
Thomas, G. S. , 1, 2, 6, 44, 59, 60
Van Dijk, J. A.
Venturi, R. , 13
Wacquant, L. , 3
Weisman, L. K. , 13
West, C. , 28, 37, 54
Will, G. , 6, 7
Wilson, E. O. , 7
Wilson, W. J., 1, 2, 3, 4
xuburbs , 3
Yiddish , 47

About the Author

Amardo Rodriguez (Ph.D., Howard University) teaches in the Department of Communication and Rhetorical Studies at Syracuse University. His research and teaching interests revolve around three questions: *How can communication theory speak better to what being human means? How can communication theory offer new vistas of what being human means? How can communication theory make for a world with less misery and suffering?*

Publications include articles in: Journal of Intercultural Communication, Journal of Intergroup Relations, Journal of Religion and Society, Southern Communication Journal, Peace Review, and elsewhere. Books include: On Matters of Liberation (I): The Case Against Hierarchy; Diversity as Liberation (II): Introducing a New Understanding of Diversity, Essays on Communication and Spirituality: Contributions to a New Discourse on Communication, and Embodying the Postcolonial Life.